CRITICAL THINKING

The Effective Beginner's Guide To Master Logical Fallacies Using A Scientific Approach And Improve Your Rational Thinking Skills With Problem-Solving Tools To Make Better Decisions

By Travis Holiday & Kevin Hollins

© Copyright 2019 By Travis Holiday & Kevin Hollins - All rights reserved.

This content is provided with the sole purpose of providing relevant information on a specific topic for which every reasonable effort has been made to ensure that it is both accurate and reasonable. Nevertheless, by purchasing this content, you consent to the fact that the author, as well as the publisher, are in no way experts on the topics contained herein, regardless of any claims as such that may be made within. As such, any suggestions or recommendations that are made within are done so purely for entertainment value. It is recommended that you always consult a professional prior to undertaking any of the advice or techniques discussed within.

This is a legally binding declaration that is considered both valid and fair by both the Committee of Publishers Association and the American Bar Association and should be considered as legally binding within the United States. The reproduction, transmission, and duplication of any of the content found herein, including any specific or extended information will be done as an illegal act regardless of the end form the information ultimately takes. This includes copied versions of the work both physical, digital, and audio unless express consent of the Publisher is provided beforehand. Any additional rights reserved.

Furthermore, the information that can be found within the pages described forthwith shall be considered both accurate and truthful when it comes to the recounting of facts.

As such, any use, correct or incorrect, of the provided information will render the Publisher free of responsibility as to the actions taken outside of their direct purview. Regardless, there are zero scenarios where the original author or the Publisher can be deemed liable in any fashion for any damages or hardships that may result from any of the information discussed herein.

Additionally, the information in the following pages is intended only for informational purposes and should thus be thought of as universal. As befitting its nature, it is presented without assurance regarding its prolonged validity or interim quality. Trademarks that are mentioned are done without written consent and can in no way be considered an endorsement from the trademark holder.

Table of Contents

- **INTRODUCTION** 18
- **CHAPTER 1: WHAT IS CRITICAL THINKING?** 21
  - TYPES OF CRITICAL THINKING 22
    - *Logical Reasoning*... 22
    - *Scientific Reasoning* 23
  - THE PSYCHOLOGY OF CRITICAL THINKING 25
  - FOUR GOALS FOR CRITICAL THINKING 25
    - *Self-direction* 25
    - *Self-discipline* 26
    - *Self-Monitoring*.. 27
    - *Self-Correction*... 27
  - HOW DO YOU IDENTIFY WHETHER OR NOT YOU ARE A GOOD CRITICAL THINKER? 28
  - HELPING YOUR CHILD THINK CRITICALLY 31
  - FIGHTING BIASES... 33
  - BIASES THAT DIRECTLY AFFECT CRITICAL THINKING 35
- **CHAPTER 2: CHARACTERISTICS OF CRITICAL THINKERS** 38
  - SEEK TO JUSTIFY THEIR BELIEFS 38
  - JUDGE THE CREDIBILITY OF SOURCES.................................... 39
  - PROCEED IN AN ORGANIZED MANNER 40
  - CLEARLY PRESENT THEIR POSITION 40
  - PROTECT THE DIGNITY OF OTHERS 41
  - ENGAGE IN OBSERVATION 41
  - SEEK CLARIFICATION 41
  - ANALYZE ARGUMENTS 42

RATIONAL 42
SELF-AWARENESS 43
HONEST 43
OPEN-MINDED 43
DISCIPLINED 44
JUDGMENTAL 44
CRITICAL THINKERS STRIVE TO BE ETHICAL AND FAIR 44
THEY HAVE TOLERANCE 45
THEY HAVE ANALYTICAL SKILLS 45
THEY EXPRESS CURIOSITY 45
THEY SEEK THE TRUTH 46
CRITICAL THINKERS POSSESS MENTAL AND EMOTIONAL FORTITUDE 46
WELL-INFORMED 47
CRITICAL THINKERS POSSESS DETERMINATION 47
CRITICAL THINKERS POSSESS INTELLECTUAL FREEDOM 48
CRITICAL THINKERS HAVE SELF-CONFIDENCE 49

CHAPTER 3: HOW TO DEVELOP CRITICAL THINKING 51
THINK AND FOCUS ON YOUR LIFE'S GOALS 52
THINK ABOUT THE CONSEQUENCES OF YOUR ACTION 53
ARGUE AND MAKE ISSUES WHEN YOU THINK THAT SOMETHING IS AMISS 53
DO NOT PUT TOO MUCH EMPHASIS ON BEING RIGHT 54
KNOW YOUR BIASES 54
KNOW THE DIFFERENCE BETWEEN WHAT YOU HAVE POWER OVER AND
WHAT YOU DO NOT 55
DO NOT RUSH THE DECISION MAKING PROCESS 56
LOOK AT A SITUATION FROM EVERY PERSPECTIVE 56
AVOID OVER ANALYZING 57
REALIZE THAT LEARNING NEVER ENDS 58
ALWAYS CONSIDER THE RISK 58

NEVER ASSUME OR JUMP TO CONCLUSIONS 59
EAT WELL 59
SEE THE OPPORTUNITY AND POSSIBILITIES AROUND YOU 60
HARNESS WASTED OR IDLE TIME 60
MAINTAIN A SKILL-TRACE JOURNAL 61
UTILIZE AND DEVELOP INTELLECTUAL STANDARDS 61
KEEN OBSERVATION 62
REASONING 62
COMMUNICATING 63

CHAPTER 4: BENEFITS OF CRITICAL THINKING 65
PROMOTES CREATIVITY 66
INITIATES SELF-REFLECTION 66
STREAMLINING THINKING 66
HELPING TO IMPROVE THE GLOBAL ECONOMY 67
HELPING TO ENHANCE EFFICIENCY IN COMMUNICATION 68
SETS THE FOUNDATION FOR SCIENCE 68
ALLOWS DEMOCRACY TO FLOURISH 69
ENHANCES PRESENTATION SKILLS 69
YOU'LL ACHIEVE THE BEST FOR YOU 70
YOU'LL IMPROVE YOUR PERFORMANCE 70
ACADEMIC PERFORMANCE 71
FOSTERS TEAMWORK 71
PROMOTES OPTIONS 72

CHAPTER 5: SKILLS FOR CRITICAL THINKING 74
INTERPRETATION 74
INFORMATION SEEKING 75
STIMULATING THINKING 76
ANALYSIS 77
NON-JUDGMENT 78

- Inference 79
- Evaluation 80
- Explanation 81
- Communication 82
- Creativity 83
- Self-regulation 84
- Using reason 85
- Reevaluation 87

CHAPTER 6: A CHECKLIST FOR ANALYZING YOUR OWN THOUGHT 90
- Is My Thinking Clear? 91
- Am I Focused? 92
- Am I Paying Attention to Questions? 93
- Am I Being Reasonable? 95

CHAPTER 7: DEVELOPING A POSITIVE MINDSET 98
- Find Your Inner Happiness 101
- Manage Your Stress 101
- Stay Motivated 102
- Prepare for Everything, Including Good Things 102
- Build A Positive Network of Contacts 103
- Accept 104
- Change your perception of things 104
- Value and respect other's ideas 105
- Assess consequences of actions or ideas 106
- Make reasoned decisions 106
- Think independently 107

CHAPTER 8: CRITICAL THINKING FOR PROBLEM SOLVING ... 109
- Step by step view of critical thinking as it applies to problem solving 110

Identify the Problem *110*
Analyze the Problem *110*
Brainstorm *111*
Decide on a Solution *111*
Take Action *111*
STRATEGIES TO IMPROVE PROBLEM SOLVING AND LOGICAL THINKING 112
Delve Deeper into the Question *112*
Make Use of Diagrams *112*
Attempt Logical Games *113*
Consider your Assumptions *113*
Choose the Right People Around You *114*
Read Logical Books *114*
Investigate Everything *115*
USE INTUITION AND CRITICAL THINKING FOR BETTER PROBLEM SOLVING 116
Think About Where Your Intuition Came From *116*
Test Your Hypothesis *117*
Try to See if You Explored All Available Options *117*
Outside the Scientific Method *118*

CHAPTER 9: CRITICAL THINKING FOR BETTER DECISION MAKING **120**
WHY DECISION MAKING IS IMPORTANT 121
DON'T TRY TO BE A PERFECTIONIST 121
DETERMINE IMPORTANT FACTORS FIRST... 122
THINK WHEN YOUR MIND IS CLEAR 123
BE SURE YOU HAVE ENOUGH TIME 123
LISTEN TO YOUR GUT 124
UNDERSTANDING COGNITIVE BIAS 125
CHOOSING YOUR TIMING WISELY 126

MAXIMIZE INSTEAD OF SETTLING 127
DECIDE ON THINGS THAT ARE IMPORTANT 127
PREDICTING THE OUTCOME 128
ESTABLISH THE FACTS 129
CONSIDER OPTIONS 129
IMPLEMENT AND EVALUATE THE OPTION 130

CHAPTER 10: REWIRING YOUR BRAIN AND CHANGING YOUR PERSPECTIVE 132
   IT IS ALL PERSPECTIVE 135
   NOT EXACTLY POSITIVE THINKING 136
   BRAIN POWER STRATEGIES TO INCREASE CRITICAL THINKING ABILITIES
   137
      Making sure that your mind has clarity. 137
      List the pros and cons of a specific action. 138
      Make sure that you are always in shape. 138
      Always see to it that you avoid bad arguments, and that you detect them. 139
      Think outside the box. 139
   HAVING AN OPEN APPROACH 140

CHAPTER 11: CRITICAL THINKING AND GOAL SETTING 144
   ALWAYS START WITH THE IDEAL SITUATION 145
   ALWAYS WRITE DOWN YOUR GOALS 145
   DETERMINE ITS IMPORTANCE 146
   YOUR GOALS SHOULD ADD SOME MEANING TO YOUR LIFE 146
   PRIORITIZE AND PURSUE YOUR GOAL 147
   SETTING A TARGET DATE 148
   TAKING SMALL STEPS 148
   LESS IS MORE 149
   MAKE A TO-DO LIST 149

- OPTION TO GO PUBLIC OR STAYING PRIVATE 150
- PLAN OF ACTION 150
- ADJUST AND ADAPT 151

CHAPTER 12: CRITICAL THINKING AND SELF-IMPROVEMENT 153

- REFLECTION 155
- SHORT-TERM VERSUS LONG-TERM GRATIFICATION 156
- SYSTEMATIC DECISION-MAKING 157

CHAPTER 13: CRITICAL THINKING AND LEADERSHIP 161

CHAPTER 14: POWERFUL STRATEGIES TO IMPROVE CRITICAL THINKING 169

- KEEP A JOURNAL 169
- SOLVE A PROBLEM EACH DAY 170
- REDEFINE YOUR VIEWPOINT 170
- QUESTION THE VIEWPOINTS OF OTHERS 171
- TAKE OUT TIME 171
- DEAL WITH ONE PROBLEM AT A TIME 171
- CHANGE YOUR PERSPECTIVE 172
- ALWAYS QUESTION ASSUMPTIONS 172
- ACKNOWLEDGE THE INFLUENCE OF GROUPS 173
- TAKE A BREATH, AND HAVE A THOUGHT 173
- TALK TO YOURSELF 174
- PRACTICE ASKING CRITICAL QUESTIONS 174
- GET VERIFIABLE EVIDENCE 175
- ASK QUESTIONS 175
- BE AWARE OF YOUR MENTAL PROCESSES 176
- FORM YOUR OWN OPINIONS 176
- DO PROPER ANALYSIS 176
- DO REASONABLE INTERPRETATION 177

CONFIRM INFORMATION VERACITY 177
DEAL WITH YOUR EGO 177
BE INNOVATIVE 178
HAVE A HEALTHY LIFESTYLE 178
BE CREATIVE 179
KNOW WHEN TO MOVE ON 179
DIVERSIFY 180
HAVE AN OPEN MIND 180
RESIST IMPULSIVENESS 181
ELIMINATE AMBIGUITY 181
BE CONSISTENT 182
PRACTICE EMPATHY 182
KNOW YOUR LEARNING STYLE 183
ELIMINATE NEGATIVE TALK 183
HAVE THE PASSION TO LEARN 184
IMPROVE LISTENING SKILLS 184
ALWAYS MAINTAIN PERSPECTIVE 185
CHECK YOUR EMOTIONS 185
DEVELOP INTELLECTUAL HUMILITY 185
STAY SELF-AWARE OF YOUR THOUGHT PROCESSES 186
ALWAYS MAKE SURE YOU'RE THINKING FOR YOURSELF 187
REMEMBER THAT NO ONE IS PERFECT 187

CHAPTER 15: CONNECTING CRITICAL THINKING TO FEELINGS FOR GREATER EMOTIONAL INTELLIGENCE 189
WHY ARE YOUR EMOTIONS IMPORTANT? 190
MAKING THE CONNECT 190
EMOTIONAL INTELLIGENCE AND CRITICAL THINKING 191
Self-Management *192*
Self-Awareness *192*

Empathy *193*
Motivation *193*
Social Skills *194*
Conflict Resolution *194*

CHAPTER 16: HOW TO BEAT HINDRANCES TO CRITICAL THINKING 197

MISSING DIRECTION 197
FEAR OF FAILURE 198
FEARING CRITICISM 199
THE STRIFE TO REMAIN CONSISTENT 199
DEFENSE MECHANISMS 200
PROCRASTINATION 200
SEEKING JUSTIFICATION 201
ENCULTURATION 201
UNFAVORABLE EMOTIONAL STATES 202

CHAPTER 17: KEEPING THE BRAIN IN SHAPE FOR CRITICAL THINKING 205

DO ENJOYABLE PHYSICAL EXERCISES 205
EXERCISE YOUR MIND 206
QUESTION THINGS 206
MAKE A POINT OF LAUGHING 207
FEED ON OMEGA 3 FATS 208
TAKE A WALK DOWN MEMORY LANE 208
REDUCE INTAKE OF SATURATED FATS 209
SOLVE PUZZLES 209
LISTEN TO YOUR BEST MUSIC 210
LIMIT YOUR ALCOHOL INTAKE 210
ENGAGE IN PLAY 211
ALLOW YOURSELF SOME SLEEP AFTER LEARNING 211

- Concentrate on what you are doing 212
- Embrace love making 213
- Put passion into your activities 213
- Keep your focus on the challenge 214

CHAPTER 18: HOW TO BECOME A CRITIC OF YOUR OWN THINKING 216
- Always Refine Your Thinking 220
- Always Stick to the Point 221
- Bravely Question All Questions Being Asked 222
- Be Rational 223

CHAPTER 19: CRITICAL THINKING IN EVERYDAY LIFE 225
- Making use of "wasted" time 228
- One problem per day 229
- Maintain an intellectual journal 229
- Reshaping your character... 230
- Dealing with your egocentrism 231
- Redefining the way in which you see things 231
- Get in touch with your emotions 232
- Analyzing the influence of a group on your life 232

CONCLUSION 235

Introduction

Critical thinking brings about excellent resolutions to problems, yet, it needs to be developed so that it can work, which requires you to have a sound strategy for success. Read on to find out how you can make critical thinking a part of your life, and how to improve your approach to problem solving and logical thinking.

In this book, you will better understand the concept of critical thinking and how you can gain the skills to become a critical thinker. The world that we live in becomes more complicated each day. You will only be able to cope with our complicated world by learning how to control your thoughts and by becoming a critical thinker.

When you can think effectively, you will realize that you can better control all aspects of your life and you can better deal with whatever problems or adversities life may throw your way. When you become a critical thinker, you will be amazed at how you can convert your aspirations into reality.

Critical thinking is always going to be important. By being a good critical thinker and mastering the skills you will learn as you read, you will become a more active learner and be in control of how much information you absorb. This is an essential skill for students in all different fields. You will also become more empathetic because you will grow to understand all different viewpoints and backgrounds.

Through this book, we will share both inspiration and practical techniques that you can use to learn and exercise critical thinking. Your life is a never-ending series of decisions. We hope that the lessons you learn from this book can equip you with the information you need to make better decisions in your life.

Read on, to start changing your life for the better today!

Chapter 1: What is Critical Thinking?

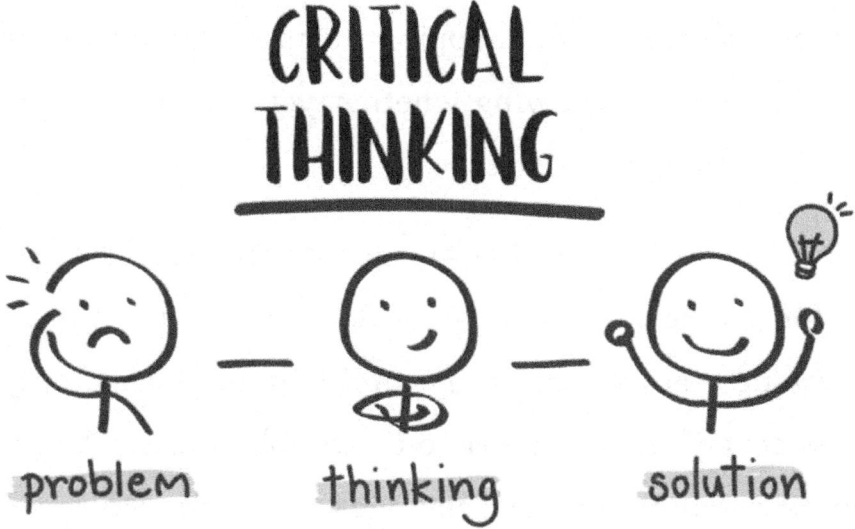

Critical thinking is a learned skill and it can benefit those who become adapt at using it in every decision they make. As a critical thinker, one of your goals is to become more familiar with your subconscious mind and to learn about the mechanics of the knowledge base that resides there. You will learn to be more introspective and reflective, meaning that you will learn to examine and consider your own mental processes including your thoughts, your emotions, and your desires.

Studying critical thinking makes you a lot smarter, and that is a fact. You would not be smarter in a subject in school, but it makes you smarter in general. For starters, it allows you to make more efficient decisions, such as choosing the right product when you are shopping, to more important global decisions such as knowing whether you should be thinking about human rights or not.

Critical thinkers know that arguments are created in such a way for people to have ways of determining the validity of everything that happens in the world. In most situations, you may not even know whether you were able to make the perfect argument in proving that a claim is valid or not. However, the way you argue would be the one that would count.

Types of critical thinking

Logical Reasoning

In its formal sense, logic is a system of rules according to which one may make inferences or draw conclusions. In other words, logic dictates how facts and conditions can be used to gain new understanding.

For example, if we begin with the factual statement that "A beagle is a type of dog," and then add the fact that "Rover is a beagle," we can then conclude that "Rover is a dog." However, if we are told "Scruffy is a dog," the laws of logic do not allow us to conclude that "Scruffy is a beagle." All beagles are dogs, but it does not follow that any dog is a beagle, so we cannot say anything else about Scruffy.

Notice that the logical example above does not show evidence for any of its claims. The facts we started with (a.k.a. "premises") are true for the sake of argument. This is why critical thinking requires evidence as well as logic, to ensure that logical claims reflect reality.

Scientific Reasoning

The scientific method is the process by which scientists and many other scholars and critical thinkers use tests and experimentation to support a claim. It is a general mode of thinking that—while primarily associated with experiments in the physical sciences such as biology, chemistry, and physics—is also prevalent in the social sciences as well as in philosophy and other disciplines.

The scientific method begins with a specific question, such as "How can I use electricity to power something?" or "Why are people suffering from this disease?" The person wishing to answer their question then provides a "hypothesis," an educated guess that they believe is possible based on what they know already. They will then conduct a test in the form of several experiments or the collection of data relevant to the problem. They may experiment with different models for harnessing electricity, compare the health records and routines of the patients living in the infected region, or simply try different brands of detergent. They then analyze their findings to draw a conclusion.

Experiments are often replicated to test results under different conditions. For example, if the experimenter found a correlation between people suffering from the same diseases in a certain area and their ingestion of a chemical in the water, they might conduct an experiment on lab animals using those chemicals, or find another population demonstrating a similar correlation and analyze them.

The Psychology of Critical Thinking

Critical thinking in psychology is defined as the habits and skills to engage in activity or exercise with reflection and criticism focusing on deciding what to believe and decisions to make. Critical thinking is a tool that is important even in psychology, and it is being taught in psychology classes. Many students coming to college have already formed theories and opinions of the subject and of life in general. When they are faced with college work, they get a shock when they find it is not what they thought it would be. Some students opt to cram the textbooks so that they will help them in the exams forgetting learning entails more than that.

Four Goals for Critical Thinking

An adept critical thinker learns that the process requires a commitment to four goals each time it is used in order to get the most out of the endeavor.

Self-direction

The first goal will be to strive for self-direction. Self-directed learning involves taking responsibility for your own acquisition and analysis of factual information from which you will learn. Your decision to dig deeper into ideas requires you to step out of your comfort zone, and you are going to have to make a decision about whether becoming a critical thinker is worth it to you. It is much easier to take things at face value – advertisers, marketers, politicians, and many others prefer that you not become a critical thinker, in fact! Most people are quite comfortable following cues from their highly conditioned subconscious mind and going about their days living in a world where they roll right along with the status quo and, quite frankly, lead mediocre lives.

Self-discipline

The second goal as a critical thinker is do develop a strong sense of self-discipline. As stated previously, learning and practicing critical thought is very challenging. Becoming a practicing critical thinker does not happen overnight and must be looked at as a process that takes a lot of introspection, self-analysis, and a commitment to change. And, if you have ever decided to learn a new skill and found it very difficult in the past, it is quite possible that you thought about giving up at some point because you found the work too hard. This is why so many New Year's resolutions are broken every year. As an example, one can visit a fitness center on January 2**nd** of any given year and usually find it to be very crowded, and visit the same fitness center forty-five days later and see a marked difference in attendance. Self-discipline is not easy.

Self-Monitoring

The third goal for a critical thinker is self-monitoring. The biases and stereotypes we have taken on in our lives are a direct result of our past experiences and the knowledge we have acquired from those experiences, as well as from what we have learned from those around us, and they may or not be accurate to some degree. Your mission as a critical thinker is to question your preconceived notions about your world and to assess and evaluate their level of accuracy as you move forward with your new ways of thought.

Self-Correction

The fourth goal a critical thinker must strive for is one of self-correction. This occurs when we reflect upon how we have perceived things in the past and then make decisions about the accuracy of those perceptions. This can be especially difficult because the knowledge base that resides in our subconscious has been hard-wired over the years. In order to have the self-discipline to correct erroneous thinking patterns (see how these goals work together?), we have to see the value of doing so. Critical thinkers will undoubtedly tell you that the benefit is that when you seek out and study various perspectives of issues, there is an opportunity for personal growth. They will also tell you, though, that questioning and correcting inaccurate perceptions that have been held throughout your life may cost you in terms of relationships. Not everyone around you will understand why you are suddenly questioning beliefs that they have held along with you for so long.

How Do You Identify Whether or Not You Are a Good Critical Thinker?

Critical thinking is a trait valued by many employers, and it is likely that they will test your critical thinking skills during the interview process. However, if this trait was not tested for, your work will show how good of a thinker you are. A weak critical thinker will begin to make costly errors. These mistakes will be repeated, which shows a lack of learning and a weak thinker will be unable to determine where action is necessary. These people will make assumptions, and the majority of their assumptions will be incorrect. This list continues to grow as better ways to evaluate a critical thinker are developed.

First, there has to be a question. It doesn't have to be impossible to answer, but it should be more complex than "What color is that car?" or "Where did you get your shirt?". Often, good questions include a political issue, but you would also use critical thinking to determine where your next move should be or what you should major in.

Second, you have to examine evidence. This won't involve pulling fingerprints or examining blood splatter samples, but you want to look at the big picture. Take on that omniscient point of view that was mentioned earlier.

Third, analyze any assumptions or biases. How does that work? Say you are talking to your friend about how her boyfriend treated her. She is upset; therefore, you can assume that she may not necessarily lay any fault in herself or she may exaggerate the situation. It's important to comfort your friend, but from a critical thinker's standpoint, you would want to consider this bias or even get the story from the boyfriend's point of view.

Fourth, remove your emotions from the situation. Like in the previous example, your friend is unable to properly evaluate the situation because she is upset and emotionally involved. This is why it is smart to go to other people for advice about big decisions. Emotions clutter and often take over the mind because, of course, we are all only human.

Fifth, when you think critically, you want to consider other interpretations. So let's talk about things from the boyfriend's point of view. Maybe what offended your friend was not intended by her boyfriend, and thus miscommunication caused the argument. This is something you should consider when trying to seriously guide your friend through this difficult time.

Sixth, sometimes, even after considering all of the information you possibly can, there are still some questions left unanswered – that's okay! Though you would like to know everything, sometimes every bit of information is hard to find. This is known as ambiguity, and to think critically, you don't need to eliminate it, but you do need to consider it.

Sometimes, what you do not know is important when it comes to decision-making. When thinking critically, you must determine the ambiguity to determine whether you even have enough information to make a clear, rational decision about a topic.

Helping Your Child Think Critically

It is easier to learn things when you are younger because many habits have not yet been formed. When you are an adult learning how to think critically, you have already spent so long thinking more simplistically that you will really have to try to think critically. For children, even toddlers, this will be a beneficial skill to learn.

You can add critical thinking to playtime. For example, when they get a new toy, instead of showing them how everything works and where the buttons that make it light up are, give them time to figure it out. At first, they will probably throw it or bang it on the floor or even take a taste test. This is okay – it is their way of learning. Once they are done with their initial evaluations, either they will give up on it and go play with a toy they know how to use, or they'll continue to investigate.

If they keep investigating, that is awesome. Their little gears are turning up there! If not, give them a nudge, give the toy back to them and ask suggestive, open-ended questions like "What is that?" or "What does this one do?". It is likely that they will respond positively to your questions. If you are excited about this new toy, they'll be excited about the new toy.

If you have asked all of the questions and given them a little more time and they are still not all the way there, now you can give them a nudge in the right direction. Now you are going to ask questions that will help them hypothesize – obviously they won't know these complex terms, but the learning process is still the same. Ask them things like "If we touch this, what will happen?". This could prompt them to press buttons or turn knobs.

You can also encourage them to think critically by talking about what you are doing. If you're playing with a light up toy, say "Let's press the button" before you press the button. Verbalizing your thought process can trigger their thought process in the same way.

It will be a very rewarding moment when your child is happy because they figured it out on their own. Their successes will make them more confident and motivated to find out how the next toy works.

Fighting Biases

Recognizing your viewpoint is as important as recognizing the viewpoints of others. This allows you to understand and limit biases. First, you should understand how to find these varying points of view. Talking to people is also useful; politics is a difficult topic to discuss, and a lot of people shy away from it when it's brought up. But if you truly want to eliminate bias, you should at least do your research.

We all know that interaction over the Internet is a million times easier than face-to-face interaction. This is detrimental in some ways, but it makes learning easier. Doing research is another way to identify different viewpoints. Bias is very apparent in everyday life, whether it is directed toward big picture things, such as the daily roles of men and women, or affording certain licenses toward people because they are famous or attractive. To think critically, you must recognize the presence of bias and eliminate it.

Being biased can be a sign that you are too close-minded or one-sided. To eliminate bias, you must practice what was outlined above. You can see that many of the things on the path to critical thinking are intertwined. Being open-minded and fair were two of the characteristics of a good critical thinker. These things will also help control and eliminate biases in a situation. A lot of the time, bias can be eliminated by removing yourself from a situation or understanding the other side's point of view. That being said, you don't necessarily have to be opinionless in this situation. You want to make an educated decision about which side of an argument you choose to eliminate bias. By being educated, you are not being one-sided because you evaluated all positions being taken which is open-mindedness.

Biases That Directly Affect Critical Thinking

There are different levels of consciousness; therefore, there can be different levels of bias. Recognizing how this affects our ability to think critically is important.

These are four common biases that can be taken out of the picture once you are aware of them:

- **Action bias**: think before you act! Critical thinking flies right out the window when you act before properly evaluating a situation.

- **Confirmation bias:** you are not always going to be right. Lots of times, you will want to take the path that will confirm what you already know. Don't – humans aren't perfect! You are not always going to be right! So while you are looking for evidence that supports your viewpoint, don't disregard the information that discredits your viewpoint. Often at times in a debate, the opposing viewpoint should be acknowledged to strengthen your argument anyway.

- **Association bias:** this can be avoided by identifying correlation versus causation. This ties into a lot of superstitious beliefs – not washing your uniform before a game and believing something bad happened on Friday the 13th because it is a day of bad luck are a couple of examples. Recognizing the difference between a coincidence and two things that are actually related will help eliminate association biases.

Chapter 2: Characteristics of Critical Thinkers

Critical thinking is made up of different skills, and its main features are as follows.

Seek to Justify Their Beliefs

Critical thinkers do not accept information at face value; they do not believe something just because others believe it. Instead, they seek to justify their decisions and beliefs. They look at hypotheses and seek alternative hypotheses in search of answers. They seek explanations and make conclusions based on evidence and facts. Critical thinkers strive to soak up information on subjects they are discussing. They look at several points of views and ensure that they give others a chance to express their viewpoints. Aim to develop this skill.

Judge the Credibility of Sources

Critical thinkers are good at judging the credibility of sources because they rely on information to make good decisions. Faulty information can change the outcome of decisions. Critical thinkers are well aware of this.

They use various factors to judge the credibility of sources to ensure that the information they receive draws on facts and evidence. Critical thinkers check expertise, reputation, and the procedures used by sources. They do not look at only one source; they do research on a variety of sources and check for agreement and disagreements. They also look at the reasons given in support of an argument.

Proceed in an Organized Manner

Critical thinkers strive to organize their thoughts and their information well before they present it to others. They are good at problem solving because they follow problem-solving steps.

They refrain from panicking when there is a problem. They know that panicking only seeks to make the situation worse. Instead of overreacting, they take stock of a situation, determine the problem, and look for ways to solve the problem. They also determine who will be responsible for carrying out which action and how they will evaluate the implementation process.

Clearly Present Their Position

Critical thinkers ensure that they present a position with honesty. They are clear in their delivery. They ensure that their audience knows their intended meaning. They discuss the issue at hand, giving information, answering questions, and offering reasons. However, they do not pretend that they know it all; they are aware that they have limited beliefs and that they can learn something from listening to others.

Protect the Dignity of Others

Critical thinkers also consider the feelings of others. They allow others to express their views. They consider the degree of sophistication and the level of knowledge that others possess and refrain from being intimidating. Critical thinkers can present the same information to people of all ages. They know how to adapt their presentation so that everyone in their audience can grasp the meaning of the topic in discussion.

Engage in Observation

Critical thinkers hone their observation skills because they know that they can derive a lot of information from observing people and situations. They not only listen to what is being said, they also observe the body language of the speaker to determine what is not being said.

Seek clarification

Critical thinkers are interested in the facts and main points. They ask questions and paraphrase in order to determine whether they have a clear picture of the situation. Critical thinkers are adept at seeking clarification; they are also adept at clarifying their points. They give definitions, explanations, facts, illustrations, and answer questions raised to ensure that everyone understands the topic in discussion.

Analyze Arguments

Critical thinkers are good at analyzing arguments. Information alone does not make one a critical thinker. You need to know what the information means. Critical thinkers seek both stated and unstated reasons when searching for answers.

They view the structure of the argument, summarize the main points, and identify the conclusions. Critical thinkers decipher relevant and irrelevant information. They can also know when a discussion is getting out of hand. They employ strategies to bring the discussion back on track and move the discussion forward.

Rational

You can say you are rational when you rely on reason and not emotion when you need evidence, and you consider that before concluding and you want to find the best explanation possible instead of just accepting whatever is given to you.

Self-awareness

You are thinking critically when you start weighing the influence your motives and bias have on the way you function and acknowledge your assumptions, perspectives and prejudices.

Honest

You can think critically once you have gained the ability to recognize your emotional impulses, your motivations or any other illusions you might have about yourself.

Open-minded

Your ability to be reasonable while evaluating inferences, of taking into consideration multiple points of views and perspectives, of being an option towards alternative interpretations, of accepting an explanation that is well-suited to accepting new priorities and of being tolerant towards yourself and others makes you open-minded.

Disciplined

Being disciplined means being able to resist irrational temptations, avoid manipulations, think clearly, avoid jumping to conclusions and be meticulous and comprehensive while functioning.

Judgmental

You will start thinking critically when you avoid being judgmental and start being rational while taking into consideration the evidence or perspectives available before forming an opinion.

Critical Thinkers strive to be Ethical and Fair

Ethical and fair critical thinkers analyze and assess their own thinking as carefully as they analyze and assess the thinking and reasoning of others. Introspective reflection can be defined as thinking about the way one uses his own mind to think. When we evaluate our own thought processes, we are looking to see how our own biases may be affecting our perspectives. In addition, we are examining how our emotions may be getting in the way of making sound decisions that could move us forward with more focus and with potentially better outcomes.

They have tolerance

In critical thinking, you need to delight at hearing varying views, as you enjoy a vibrant debate and are an active listener.

They have analytical skills

Critical thinkers, of necessity, must have analytical skills, and if you do not have them you need to develop them. You are not expected to be one of those people who accept whatever has been said without thinking or taking a minute to analyze it. Critical thinkers prefer to construct arguments properly, and also to come up with sound reasons, before they can make any conclusions. Once you have analyzed the problem well, the conclusions you draw are bound to be sound.

They express curiosity

Critical thinkers are curious people. After all, how are you going to learn if you are not eager to know what is happening? Curiosity, in the context of critical thinking, is a basic ingredient in the acquisition and development of ideas as well as insights.

They seek the truth

You can only be a great critical thinker if you seek to establish the truth and validity of information before drawing your conclusions. In fact, critical thinkers who are worth their salt do not worry that once they establish what the truth is, it might end up negating the premise they earlier held. Instead, they are prepared to replace their earlier convictions, if they happen to be unfounded, with the objective truth. In doing this, critical thinkers do not work for their own interest but for the common good.

Critical Thinkers Possess Mental and Emotional Fortitude

Mental and emotional fortitude come into play when we become critical thinkers because it's not easy to begin to question beliefs we have held our entire lives. It may seem much easier to avoid the work in front of us, which includes examining our own patterns of thought and behavior and considering what is true and what is not based upon the evidence we find. What will it mean if you come to the conclusion that a strong belief you have had since childhood turns out to be false? How will you handle that new information, and what will it mean to have to adjust your life accordingly? One has to possess courage in order to do the work required of a critical thinker because of what one may discover about past beliefs.

Well-Informed

Critical thinking revolves around making informed decisions. You cannot make informed decisions based on scanty information or knowledge. As a critical thinker, you must prioritize information gathering. If your knowledge on a specific subject is lacking, desist from making a decision, and proceed to gather relevant information (become well informed) on it before making a decision.

Critical Thinkers Possess Determination

You will read throughout this book that thinking critically is not always easy, particularly in the beginning when the concepts involved in critical thinking are new to you. The other fact that makes critical thinking a challenge is that not many people are aware of what it means to be a critical thinker, and thus do not practice it. Just like any other new skill you may learn in your life, critical thought takes a lot of practice to become skilled at it, and you will hit your roadblocks. When you get stuck, or feel like slipping into your old ways of thinking, you must get in touch with why you took up the study of critical thinking in the first place and reconnect with your motivation. Those who become practicing critical thinkers reap benefits that the rest of the world do not realize.

Critical Thinkers Possess Intellectual Freedom

One of the most important qualities that a critical thinker enjoys is the autonomy to think for himself. People who do not learn to think critically often have their opinions and ideas shaped by others, or are so bound by their biases that they shun the opinions of others. Strong thinkers who learn to apply the concepts of critical thought in their lives realize that they have the freedom to think for themselves and make their own decisions independent of influences like past bias, the media, the government, or others around them. Intellectual freedom is powerful because it helps the critical thinker find the truth, or at least develop an opinion that has been made by systematically researching all perspectives.

Critical Thinkers have Self-Confidence

Once you begin to work with your new critical thinking skills, you will develop confidence in your thinking processes because you will know that they are systematic and sound. This does not mean that all of your problem-solving from this point forward will be easy, because you will still have to wrestle with your emotions if they conflict with your logic in terms of making a particular decision. However, if you use your critical thinking skills to help solve your problems or to answer important questions that you must ask, you will have the confidence and satisfaction knowing that you have considered all of the options available to you in a systematic and thorough way.

Chapter 3: How To Develop Critical Thinking

As long as you are alive, you will have thoughts, and make decisions each day of your life. As long as you are alive, it is never too late to develop critical thinking and become a critical thinker.

We have great capacity to accomplish certain tasks and activities. In fact, those who lack talent in specific areas can hone their talents through practice. The same goes for critical thinking.

You can use the below strategies to develop critical thinking skills.

Think and focus on your life's goals

Everybody has a purpose, but most people make the worst decisions because they lose sight of their goals. Ask yourself this: Why do I want to continue waking up and working hard?

Knowing what your goals are will almost instantly give you all the insights that you need to reach them, because your mind is wired to do that. You would know that you need to make certain steps in order to see to it that you achieve the things that you are set to have. At the same time, your goals will also define every decision that you make. If one of your major goals is to buy a house before you reach 30, then that would make you decide to get a job and create a savings account.

Think about the consequences of your action

To be a critical thinker, you need to always consciously think about what is very likely to happen after you make a decision. By doing this, you immediately become concerned if your actions will backfire or would they give you more benefit. Also consider other viewpoints that would allow you to see the entire picture, and in any case that you missed giving a more beneficial decision, chalk it to experience. By being aware of what could have happened, you would know how to act better the next time you encounter that situation.

Argue and make issues when you think that something is amiss

If your intuition tells you that a specific brand of toothpaste is not really going to make your teeth become pearly white, then you have every reason to question how it is advertised. When you think about it, this is how you check every doubt that you have in mind. When you practice critical thinking, you would begin to see the world as it really is.

Do Not Put Too Much Emphasis on Being Right

Critical thinkers can realize that they do not have to be right all the time or have all of the answers. Being a critical thinker means taking all information into consideration before making a decision. Therefore, if you do not know something, do not be afraid to accept and change that thought. Asking questions is important, and is something that you should never be afraid of as a critical thinker. Do not make any judgment or decision if you do not know enough information to do so. Critical thinking involves making the right decision, more than being right all the time.

Know Your Biases

As human beings, we all have certain issues that stir up passion in us. This is important to take into consideration when you are trying to master the critical thinking skill. Again, having strong feelings about one issue or another is not out of the ordinary, rather it is quite normal. But making decisions on topics which cause your thinking processes to be clouded by emotion can become a problem in terms of thinking critically.

Thus, you should keep in mind what issues might cause you to be biased or prejudiced in some way. Once you know what those issues are, you can take time to evaluate your thoughts and understand why you are so affected by them. This can help in many ways, including enabling you to articulately explain your opinions to others, and pushing you to think twice or three times before making a final decision that is relative to this issue.

Know the Difference Between What You Have Power Over and What You Do Not

Thinking critically is all about being efficient. Not being able to acknowledge what elements of a situation are within your power to change can hinder the efficiency of your thoughts. Trying to change things that are not in your sphere of influence can cause you to waste a lot of time and energy. Taking the time to evaluate all of the elements of the issue and noting which of them you can control, will help you to use your valuable time and energy in a way that is productive. Any elements that are not under you control are not your concern, and not worth the effort to think about more than is absolutely necessary.

Do Not Rush the Decision Making Process

One of the biggest factors that affect our ability to make well informed and solid decisions is the constraint of time. It is true, that often when making a personal or professional decision, there is a limit to how much time we have before we must make a decision and act upon it. Even so, try to take as much time as you need so that you are able to make the right decision. Rushing the critical thinking process can lead to a host of issues.

Look at a Situation from Every Perspective

Thinking is quite an individual activity indeed, but often, the more people that participate in coming to a conclusion, the more successful the outcome is. By consulting with others, you will get many perspectives on the same situation because everyone will be bringing his or her own experience to the table.

As a critical thinker, you should realize that the view of a situation you have is going to be partial and biased, no matter what you do. There are always other perspectives to take into consideration which will reveal important aspects of the situation. One way to take advantage of this is to put yourself in the position of a person with whom you may have a conflict or feel the need to criticize.

Avoid Over Analyzing

When making decisions, there is such a thing as analyzing too much. While analysis is a very important part of thinking critically, over-analyzing can lead to paralysis when making decisions. Experience critical thinkers are able to analyze data while not falling into the trap of trying to force their information to fit one particular outcome or need. There is no way that you will be able to get as much information as you possibly can, because there is an infinite amount of information available. But, once you know that you have gotten all of the information that you can and you have looked at that information thoroughly, with an objective point of view, you should be able to move forward towards making sound decisions.

Realize that Learning Never Ends

Another important habit for being a critical thinker is to always be on the move, looking for more information, on a wide variety of topics and issues. Thinking critically will be greatly enhanced by having more information at hand. In order to maintain this habit, you should constantly make an effort to read and further your information, as you never know what information will be beneficial in terms of future decision making.

Always Consider the Risk

Everything we do in life is based on navigating the prospect of certain risks. Often, risks are behind the preventative measures that we take for granted in our day to day life. Critical thinkers will do more than just prepare to deal with a risk in the event that it should happen. Rather, they will take any action necessary to prevent the situation in which people fall victim to said risk.

Never Assume or Jump to Conclusions

Critical thinkers make a habit of never jumping to conclusions. At times, it seems like the solution to a problem is obvious, and when that is the case you may want to go with the first conclusion that comes to mind. However, the obvious solution is not always the best. Before you take action, make sure to look at all of the presented evidence and think carefully about what the best solution might be. Critical thinkers come to conclusions based on evidence, not vice versa. Taking the time to gather as much information as possible will aid your ability to understand a complicated situation before taking actions, which may not be the best ones to take.

Eat Well

This may come as a shock, but critical thinking ability can be affected by what we take into our bodies as well as our mind. In order to make sure that your brain is at its sharpest, there are a few eating habits that should be kept in mind.

See the opportunity and possibilities around you

You can't always say that there is only one approach to solve a problem. At the same time, you cannot always say that a problem is just a problem. When you think about it, a problem may be introduced to you as a nerve-wracking dilemma, but it may be an opportunity in disguise.

Critical thinkers are often mistaken to be optimistic, but that is hardly true. They do not see the world as a bleak and sorry place to be in, because they know that there are always an easy way to solve problems. Sometimes, they even welcome problems because it provides them the avenue to be creative and use a dire situation to their advantage.

Harness Wasted or Idle Time

You possess the ability to waste, or utilize time well. Unfortunately, many of us spend a majority of our time watching television. Often, we usually do not have a particular show we are following; we just surf through the channels to see what is available.

The thing about time is that once it is gone, it is gone for good. You will not get back that time. Often times, you may complain that you do not have enough time, but when asked about what you managed to accomplish, you are at a loss for words.

Maintain A Skill-Trace Journal

Thinking about how you employed critical thinking and the steps involved is good, but it is not enough. Go a step further and note down the process in a journal. Something about journaling brings forth often hidden feelings and thoughts.

Utilize and Develop Intellectual Standards

Accuracy, breadth, clarity, depth, precision, logicalness, relevance, and significance are universal intellectual standards that every critical thinker should strive to develop. The best way to go about developing these standards is to practice one intellectual standard per week. This way, you will be able to master one standard before moving on to the next one.

During your practice, you should be able to focus on stating, elaborating, illustrating, and exemplifying the standard. This way, you will be able to cover all your bases.

Keen observation

Observation is central to any analytical process, and it is actually what you do first and foremost. As a matter of fact, human beings keep observing things and happenings around them, sometimes just accidentally and, at other times, as a deliberate move in their critical observation.

Reasoning

Reasoning is how you think and how you understand issues so that you are able to derive conclusions or make judgments. Reasoning is based on logic, and it is also based on available evidence.

Even when you are learning in school, you appreciate things better when you can reason, because you can go through facts and supporting evidence and come to a logical conclusion as to why things happen in a certain way, or why things in the past happened as they did. It is reasoning that helps you decide what to take in as important in your life, and what to relegate to the back burner. It supports your critical thinking process, leading you to gathering your different thoughts as well as any information you have, in preparation to taking any steps you may deem necessary. In short, reasoning helps you to have a better understanding of the issue at hand.

Communicating

You can take communicating to be the exchange of thoughts as well as information between parties. Is this not what you do almost on a continuous basis? Although you may have taken that for granted, you may appreciate that serious topics tend to go smoothly whenever you have thought critically about what to say before actually saying it.

Chapter 4: Benefits of Critical Thinking

Putting aside value judgment about how anyone should live their lives, the following are a few practical benefits to incorporating critical thinking into your life:

Promotes Creativity

Creativity and critical thinking are two pieces in a pond. Here is how the two relate. To come up with something new, or to make something old better, you first need to study it, and form an opinion or idea on how to go about it.

Initiates Self-Reflection

To achieve growth, and live a meaningful life, you must shine light on what drives you, what is important to you as an individual, and how that relates to the world at large. Critical thinking enables you to reflect on your values and the values of your decisions. You will not 'hide from yourself'; instead, you will engage in self-evaluation, which will go a long way in helping you determine choices and decisions you make in your life.

Streamlining thinking

By streamlining what is meant is giving your thinking direction. You will appreciate how important this is when you consider that you, very likely, do not have the monopoly of certain information on which you are basing your arguments. As such, it is what you have as your values and your level of competence as a critical thinker that determine the kind of argument you come up with, and how helpful that argument will be to all involved.

Helping to improve the global economy

When you are dealing with market forces today and resources that are available, and also the locations where those resources are found, you need to have the data available that is well analyzed in order to form useful information. Critical thinking is central to this process, otherwise you would have resources underutilized, others over-employed and yet others misused. With critical thinking, for example, you get to determine whether it is viable to put up a factory in one location or another, and if it is economical to use labor-intensive methods of production as opposed to mechanical based processes.

Helping to enhance efficiency in communication

In critical thinking, you get to organize data in a way that gives a sensible picture of something or a situation, one that helps you to form an opinion, and even make a decision based on that picture. In critical thinking, you also get to analyze and assess data, with a view to forming a well thought out opinion regarding the situation. In short, you can only present an idea with valid arguments when you have been engaged in critical thinking.

Sets the Foundation for Science

Without critical thinking, it would be impossible to make advancements in science and technology. When it comes to questioning theories and searching for answers (thinking critically), scientists and researchers are at the forefront. Science relies on critical thinkers to come up with formulas and answers; it relies on data and proof of concept, concepts that call for critical thinking.

Allows Democracy to Flourish

True democracy flourishes when individuals can voice opinions, ask questions, and seek answers. Democracy provides governmental checks and balances; it allows citizens of a country to hold their leaders accountable. We often fight not because we disagree but because we feel as if our concerns are being neglected or trivialized. Critical thinking allows people from all occupations to look at issues from various angles, and arrive at the best possible solution.

Enhances Presentation Skills

Life may call upon you to give a presentation at work, school, at a seminar, during a course, at a religious gathering, or even at a family meeting. To give a great presentation, you need to employ critical thinking. Critical thinking equips you with the skills to give clear and systematic presentations where you state your points, give the reasoning behind your points, and provide proof for your stand on specific subjects. By using critical thinking, when called to do so, you are also able to defend your position. When giving a presentation, you should use various resources such as graphs, charts and images to get your points across.

You'll Achieve the Best for You

While certain academic disciplines and professions are popularly associated with critical thinking, it actually transcends any one subject or function. Critical thinking represents a deeper examination of things, understanding problems, situations, questions, and even people on a much more substantive level. It can be applied in a number of areas in your own life—allowing you to analyze and evaluate an important decision or a lengthy project according to the facts and move forward with confidence.

You'll Improve Your Performance

Professional development courses, executive training, and other programs aimed at improving productivity all teach some form of critical thinking. They may use different terms or apply it to different situations, but they all rely upon self-awareness, clear thinking, and rational analysis as tools to "get ahead" in the workplace. Regardless of your job, critical thinking can make your work easier and increase productivity, which are good things for both you and your boss!

Academic performance

Instead of depending on teachers and classroom for instructions, students that have critical thinking skills are independent and self-directed learners. They are also able to evaluate the way they learn, examine the areas where they're strong and weak, and lead the path they wish to take in school.

Fosters Teamwork

Every person in the entire workforce can get involved in solving problems through the application of the critical thinking process. This is where brainstorming comes in in an organization. When more people are involved, more solutions or ideas are presented. In the workplace, there are people from diverse backgrounds, and they can come together each giving their own idea based on their understanding, experience, and expertise. This fosters teamwork as different employees come together to find a solution through working together. Employees feel appreciated and feel that they have been given a chance to impact the future of the organization. Critical thinking promotes tolerance in the workplace and understanding.

Promotes Options

The advantage of critical thinking in the workplace is that the company is able to develop many viable solutions to the same problem. This promotes workplace innovation as well as being able to offer varied solutions to clients. Having several solutions to a problem in a company allows your company to use available resources instead of purchasing new materials. This will save money for your company, and customers will benefit from having a variety of solutions to choose from.

Chapter 5: Skills for Critical Thinking

Interpretation

This not only includes the ability to understand the information that you have been presented with but also includes your ability to be able to communicate its meaning to others. You will find yourself in different situations where you will need to make use of this critical skill. Interpretational skills will help you in getting a better understanding of the information that you have been presented with, and it also helps in decoding the same. Doing this will provide you some clarity.

Application exercise: Make a list of 10 facial expressions that can be equated to different emotions. For instance, a smile means happiness; a frown can mean confusion and so on. Try analyzing the different emotions you can gauge by looking at someone else's expressions.

Information Seeking

Critical thinking is about taking the facts and combining them with what you know to create perspective. This perspective helps you decide based on what you have learned and any other factors that come into play. The importance of logic in critical thinking makes information seeking a big part of the critical thinking process. This is especially true since the knowledge that you have affects your perspective, as well as the variety of the options available to you.

Application exercise: Imagine that your boss comes to you with a big project—working with the budgeting department to implement an energy-saving plan for the company. The goal is to maximize the benefits while spending as little on equipment and energy-saving alternatives as possible.

As the field of energy technology is rapidly expanding, this is something that you will want to research before diving into it. Carry out research and come up with an energy-saving plan that is effective, but cost-friendly.

Stimulating Thinking

There are opportunities all around you that you can use to practice critical thinking through your day. For example, when your coworker asks you to complete their assignment over the weekend, you have to critically think about it. Consider if you would be sacrificing something, like plans you had previously made. Then, think about the coworker and if there are any benefits. There are times when you can (and should) help others without expecting anything back, but it should not be a one-sided relationship. Be kind, but do not be afraid to say no, whether you had plans or just wanted to relax over the weekend. Answering them should not be an instantaneous response—take the time to critically think. By taking advantage of situations like these, you are getting the practice you need to become 'good' at critical thinking.

Application exercise: One of the easiest ways to stimulate critical thinking is by asking yourself questions about a scenario. Ask things like, 'What is my point of view on this topic?' and 'Why do I believe that?' Answer these questions and identify your reasoning for your point of view and consider any alternative perspectives that might exist. This process can be applied to any scenario in your life to create a critical thinking situation.

Analysis

Being able to connect the different pieces of information that you have been provided with and determining the intended meaning of the same is known as analysis. This skill lends its user the ability to read between the lines and will help you in understanding the actual meaning of something. Analysis is an easy skill to acquire, but it does take a while to master.

Application exercise: If you are interested in starting to practice this skill, then try to understand the meaning of this Chinese proverb "Be the first to the field and the last to the couch." Did you understand what this proverb is trying to convey? We will obviously all have a different interpretation, but this proverb is essentially talking about hard work.

Non-Judgment

It is essential for critical thinkers to view different perspectives without being judgmental. Critical thinking requires you to consider different viewpoints in a way that is objective, taking in the knowledge without emotionally charging it or manipulating it to fit your agenda. It is easy to let emotions cloud judgment, especially when you are passionate about your topic. However, if you let bias cloud your view, then you can never be sure if the conclusion you have drawn comes from the facts or the emotions in the situation.

Application exercise: Practicing mindfulness helps you learn how to acknowledge your thoughts without letting them cloud your judgment. Start by bringing your mind to a state of focus and relaxation. Sit in a quiet room and take some deep breaths, paying attention to the feeling of your belly falling and rising. Once you feel relaxed, open your eyes and choose a point of focus. You can watch a beetle on the windowsill, observe the wood patterns on your desk, or look at a painting on the wall. Look at your chosen point of focus and observe it without analyzing it or judging it in any way. If you do think something, observe the thought without becoming emotionally attached to it. Focus on your breaths again until your mind clears and return to your main point of focus.

Inference

The ability to conclude by understanding and recognizing the different elements that you are presented with is known as inference. Well, most people tend to jump to a conclusion without taking into consideration all the information that is available. Doing this will lead to faulty assumptions and, in turn, it can affect your ability to take decisions. Think of a scenario where you are the business manager, and you are looking at the sales forecast. You notice that the sales have dropped. It is essential that you can take into consideration other additional information to determine the exact reason for the decrease in sales. There can be internal and external issues that led to the decline in the sales.

Application exercise: Select a crime show and watch one episode per week. Notice and observe the different clues that they drop and see if you can figure out on your own who the culprit is, before the end of the show. This will help you with your inferential skills.

Evaluation

This refers to the skill of being able to evaluate the credibility of a statement or the information that you have been presented. This skill comes in handy when you have measured the validity of the information on hand.

Application exercise: There is a very easy way in which you can hone this skill. Just open your laptop and search for tests for evaluation skills and voila! You will have plenty of tests to choose from, and this will help you in developing your evaluation skills.

Explanation

Explanation is the skill of being able to restate the information in such a way that it adds clarity and perspective to it. This is needed so that such information can be adequately understood. For instance, think of a scenario where you have to give two presentations about a new product idea - one for the board of directors of the company and other to the product engineers. Both the parties will be keen on listening to what you have to say. However, the way you present the information before these two groups will be significantly different. The board will probably be interested in only the high-level idea whereas the team of product engineers will be interested in learning about the specific details of the product. Your ability to explain your idea while taking into consideration the audience you are presenting to is quintessential to make sure that the information is not just well received but is understood as well.

Application exercise: A really simple way in which you can hone this skill is by explaining a rather complicated concept to two different people. You can use your kids and your spouse for this. The way you explain a particular concept to your spouse will be different from the way in which you will explain it to your children. The goal is quite simple - the audience should understand what you are saying.

Communication

One commonly overlooked skill in the art of critical thinking is communication. Even the most intelligent, introverted individuals have to communicate to be successful at critical thinking.

Communication is useful in many stages of the critical thinking process. During the information seeking stage, you might need to speak to or communicate with others to ask about research they have done or their knowledge on the subject you are studying. Communicating with others can also help you learn about other perspectives or ideas that are relevant, which is important for coming up with alternative choices. Even after you have finished researching your ideas, it is important to use communication to share what you have learned. This is true whether your idea was a success or not—sharing gives everyone the opportunity to learn from your thoughts and ideas.

Application exercise: Next time you critically think about an idea, take the time to thoroughly research it and come up with different perspectives. Use what you have learned to create a PowerPoint presentation, as if you were going to give a slideshow presentation and explain the idea and different perspectives that exist.

Creativity

Some people overlook creativity as an important trait, especially for something like critical thinking that focuses on logical thought. Even so, critical thinking requires creativity when coming up with alternatives and problem solving. It is essential and as simple as knowing when to step outside of the box and come up with an unconventional solution. Being creative broadens your perspective and gives you greater insight into the possibilities of the world.

Have you ever noticed that children are more likely to be in touch with their imagination than adults? As we age, we are often told that we should focus on logic and completing our studies. This can be beneficial to intelligence—but intelligence is worth nothing unless you have the ability and creativity that are necessary to use it. Over time, focusing our brains away from the creative side of things causes our mind to disregard creative ideas before we consciously have them. This means that even though our minds are still capable of creative thought, we are not receiving the ideas in our conscious mind. It is like a phone call going through to a line with no service—the connection to that creative thought cannot be completed.

Application exercise: Fostering creativity in your life is as simple as getting in the habit of trying new things. Take a dance class or order something new at a restaurant. Creative thought can also be benefited through creative acts, like sewing, crafting, painting, writing, playing a musical instrument, singing, or any other number of activities.

Self-regulation

This refers to having an awareness of your thinking process and the elements that you make use of for finding the results that you did. Self-regulation is important because it helps you avoid bias in your thinking. For example, imagine that you are trying to convince one of your parents to try a new pharmaceutical drug that can help treat their heart disease. If you are trying to convince them to take the medicine, you might look up the positives for the drug and fail to look up the possible side effects. This gives you a limited view and makes your thinking process (and the conclusions you draw) invalid.

Application exercise: Imagine that you are on a call with a customer and are trying to help the customer fix a problem with the company's software that they are using. Also, this is your first week at the job. The problem that you are trying to rectify is a difficult one, but you want to assist the customer in making a good impression. Well, the ideal thing to do is to transfer that call to a coworker with prior experience in the same, and this will help the customer obtain the best results. This is about learning to differentiate between your personal biases while making a decision related to your work. Don't let your self-interests hinder your ability to decide what is best for your work.

Using reason

At the foundation of critical thinking is reasoning. Even if you are making a decision that involves emotion, you must keep your thinking rational and reasonable. For example, a person may stay in a relationship based on the rationale that the other person loves them or needs them. It is even possible they have grown to love the other person, even though they are abusive. In this case, emotional thinking is harmful because within any rational thought, the only logical solution is to leave the relationship.

Reasoning involves using rational, factual pieces of information to reach your conclusion. It involves using the logical side of the brain rather than the emotional and basing your conclusions on knowledge instead of feelings. This gives you the goal of thinking clearly and making sounder decisions.

Application exercise: Envision a scenario where someone you are close to, like a sibling, friend, or significant other, comes to you with a problem. The problem is illegal, unethical, or otherwise undesirable to be in.

Think of different scenarios that result from this incident. For example, if someone close to you says that they killed someone, some potential outcomes would be trying to cover it up or calling the police to report the scenario. Think of factors that might lead to each of these decisions. For example, how the person was killed. Then, imagine the results and how it would affect everyone involved. Think about the way that logic and emotion affected the decision in each of the scenarios.

Reevaluation

Critical thinkers understand that knowledge is not absolute. Technology is constantly advancing, and the field of science is researching and pushing further each day to give us a deeper and greater understanding of the world around us.

As new information becomes available, it is important to reevaluate what you know and what you have learned. Look at new information objectively, to determine if decisions you have made, or your viewpoint is going to change. By keeping current on the decisions that you make that influence your life, you are continuing on the path toward meeting your goals.

Application exercise: Choose a topic that you are passionate about and do research, looking for sources that are at least 10-20 years old. Gather information using these older sources. Then, do a search for newer information on your chosen topic. Evaluate how much the field has changed in just 10-20 years.

This showcases how important it is to always stay current with information before making decisions.

Well, these skills can be cultivated quite easily, but if you want to master them, then you will need to put in considerable time and effort for doing the same. This practice will give you the confidence that you need to successfully use these skills in your daily life.

Chapter 6: A checklist for Analyzing Your Own Thought

In order to elevate your thinking so that you can become a successful thinker, you must know about the way that you think. For many people, thinking about their own thoughts is the last thing they would ever do. However, a large part of thinking critically is knowing about the way that you think and analyzing it in order to improve it.

Analyzing one's thoughts is not an easy process, and some may even find it unpleasant and painful, but it as challenge that is worth rising to if you want to be a skilled critical thinker. In this chapter, you will find a list of questions that you can ask yourself in order to discipline your mind and ultimately become a much more reasonable person.

Is My Thinking Clear?

The human brain processes a seemingly infinite amount of information, each day, by instinct. However, if you were to scrutinize what people actually think about relative to the information that they receive, you will realize that most people have a lot of vague thoughts. Most people's thoughts seem clear to them, even when they are not, but in order to develop your mind, you must be able to clarify your thinking and make your thoughts more precise.

For instance, when you are listening to someone or even reading a new story, try to understand the real meaning of what you are hearing or reading. Explain what you understand about an issue to others in order to help yourself make the thought clear in your own mind.

In addition, when someone says something to you, you can try to summarize what they have said in your own words and ask them whether you understood them correctly. You may be shocked at the number of times that you do not understand exactly what someone is trying to communicate to you each day! When it comes to critical thinking, however, there is no room for guessing.

When speaking to others, clarify your thinking by articulating exactly what you mean. Some strategies to follow include saying one point at a time, then elaborating on it. Next, you can give examples of what you are thinking so that others can connect your thoughts to their own experience, and even use metaphors or other figurative language to make people connect your ideas to other things which they already understand, thus making your point even more clear.

Am I Focused?

Another thing to check for when analyzing one's thinking is thoughts that do not have any logical connections, and are not relevant. When solving a problem, do not allow your mind to wander. Fight the urge to think about things that are not related to the main issue, and discourage others from doing this as well. When your thinking drifts away from the topic at hand, regain control. Disciplined thinking is able to stop thoughts from thinking about things that are not pertinent and making the mind concentrate only on the things that it needs to find a solution.

Am I Paying Attention to Questions?

This question is not only about the questions that you may be asked. It also covers scrutinizing the questions that you ask and the ones that you do not as well. You should be listening to the way other people formulate their questions as well as when or why they ask certain questions.

In addition, when it is your turn to ask questions, you should take a close look at the kinds of questions that you should ask and the kinds of questions that you actually ask. It is also important to know whether you ask enough questions, or whether you are just a complacent listener who accepts blindly what others present to you.

Most people fall into this last category, accepting everything as it is presented to them and not taking the time to ask thoughtful questions. Even when most people do ask questions, they are often superficial, and do not help to solve a problem or inform a decision. As a critical thinker, the questions that you ask should help you to understand and deal with the world around you. You should be asking questions that will bring real issues to the forefront and that are powerful.

In order to become more powerful when it comes to formulating questions, you can start by always asking a question to clarify when you do not understand something. Also, when you are dealing with a complex problem, you should try to rephrase the question that you are trying to come up with an answer to in many different ways, in order to find one that is most appropriate for addressing the current problem. Finally, when you are planning to discuss an issue, you should write a list of the most important questions that need to be addressed during the discussion in order to keep the dialogue focused and clear.

Am I Being Reasonable?

A very important thing to be able to keep in check when it comes to your thoughts unreasonable behaviors. As human beings, we are quite emotional creatures, and even the most successful critical thinkers have moments of weakness in which they forgo reason when thinking about things.

You should notice whenever you are not willing to listen to the opinions of those around you, and you think that you are right and everyone else is wrong. Always ask yourself whether the viewpoints of others might have any value or merit, and whether or not you are really hearing what they are saying.

You should also beware of unreasonable behavior in other people. A good critical thinker has no problem changing his or her views, when given good reason to do so. When you discover a better way of thinking, you should never let pride prevent you from adapting your own way. In order to become more reasonable, you should always remind yourself that you are not perfect, you make mistakes and you are often wrong. You should have the courage to admit these facts if you are in a disagreement.

You should also realize the signs that you may be close minded. If you are unwilling to listen to another person's reasoning, are irritated when doing so and become defensive during discussions, then you need to re-evaluate your thinking process. If you do find that you have been unreasonable, then you should analyze why you were thinking in that manner by asking your self why you were close minded in the situation, what thinking you were trying to hold on to and what thinking is potentially better than that.

The best thinkers are those who are able to discipline their thoughts and analyze their thinking process. They realize that it is important to learn about and know one's own mind, thoughts, feelings and desires. As a budding critical thinker, you must accept these facts as well.

Chapter 7: Developing A Positive Mindset

Complaining is part of human nature. The problem is in living complaining about everything. Then the person is only thinking and vibrating negatively. And, like everything in the Universe and governed by the Law of Attraction, what you think, do, and speak will be attracted and can be realized in life.

He who emanates negative thinking will generate more negative energy, will attract more negativity and will materialize and live in negative situations. So we have to think positively.

Our mind has to believe, feel and have positive thoughts. It is with a positive mind that we will attract good energies, live in more positive environments and begin to have opportunities to realize our goals and dreams. Positive Mind is nothing more than using the Law of Attraction to attract to our life what we desire: love, prosperity, travel, health, joy, luck and so many dreams and goals.

And the most interesting of all is that the energy we draw from the Universe to generate positivism or negativity in our lives is the same. The Universal or Vital Energy is an inexhaustible source that only generates Pure Energy for whom it wishes to attract to his life through the power in the mind.

What makes energy good or bad in a person's life is the thought of it. In other words, you always attract energy. The form as this energy will manifest in your life will depend on your vibration.

Positive thinking is the first step of a long journey for you to be happier and achieve your positivity. There are no miracles. There is a need for changes in habits and thoughts to start a new life.

Start by changing your negative or stagnant mental programming and you do start to think positively. You will notice that you will begin to attract new opportunities and more positive people into your life.

Then we can understand that a positive mindset is a set of actions that lead to the realization of a desire through positive thoughts. However, for the realization of the selected desires, the mental procedure must be totally 100% positive. If only one thought, simple, short, negative, will be enough to maculate the whole procedure, and so the expected result will not be achieved.

To help you stay optimistic and positive, look at these 5 practices:

Find Your Inner Happiness

We all have something that makes us move forward, that animates us, gives us strength and serves as propelling energy for our actions. It can be family, love, success, faith, a hobby, travel, *etc*. Whatever causes you this sensation, enjoy it. Cultivate this daily within you and cling to what keeps you walking. Put a reminder or symbol that refers to what makes you happy in one place you can see daily, not to forget and stay inspired.

Manage Your Stress

The way you deal with your stress can save or sink you, depending on what it is. Even at lower levels, stress can cause physical and psychological problems, such as headaches, exhaustion, high blood pressure, gastrointestinal problems, the feeling of disability, and depression.

Each person has different ways to relieve stress, so find the one that works for you. Singing, painting, dancing, writing, doing physical exercises, listening to music, and meditating are some effective and popular ways to combat discouragement. Always reserve space in your calendar for some enjoyable activity.

Stay Motivated

Often, when we go through a long process, such as having a business of our own, we forget the reasons why we are doing certain things. Always remember what motivated you to begin, what goals you have already achieved, which ones you still want to win, and what your biggest prize is. And then stay focused.

Success takes time, persistence, and trust. Many people try thousands of times before they can. Remember: even if you have tried several times, the next one may be the right one!

Prepare for Everything, Including Good Things

We cannot predict what will happen, so always be prepared. Yes, bad things can happen, as well as good things, and you have to be ready to take advantage of them. Be open-minded and do not let negative events tear you down. And if that happens, get up! You will encounter obstacles and make mistakes, so accept them and learn from them.

You will also find joys, opportunities and various wonderful situations. Also make sure you are ready to grab the opportunities, live your dreams and get the best out of it.

Build A Positive Network of Contacts

We tend to approach people with the same vision and attitude as ourselves, and this can be both good and bad. If you have a negative view of the world, you may end up approaching people who think the same way and even if they do not want to, they will let you down because they can not see a solution either.

On the other hand, if you get along with more optimistic and confident people, they will help you to always see a positive response, solution or action. Of course, you do not have to take people out of your life, but create a network of contacts that you can trust and find motivation!

Accept

Yes, we need to accept that problems lie in our thinking. It is a need to say yes to the challenge in improving our thinking. Sometimes our ego and pride hinder us from committing to learning; we likewise need to get rid of these to begin regular practice. So, ask yourself over and over again, do you fully accept that you were once an unreflective thinker? If you consistently answer yes, then you are ready.

Change your perception of things

In every situation, we are the ones who give meaning to it. Your current status can be transformed by the way you see it. You have the power in your mind to make your life more fulfilling. A problem is only a problem when you see it as a problem. You can give it either negative or positive definitions. We are sad when we could be happy. We are frustrated when we could be fulfilled. Changing our perception of things will redefine negative thoughts into positive ones, problems as blessings, and regrets and mistakes into chances for growth. The drill is to set a specific guideline for us.

Value and respect other's ideas

Critical thinking is not always about thinking about your personal interest and will for that is a different thing called ego. A true and developed thinker values and respects the ideas of others sincerely. It is a form of humility and another aspect of critical thinking.

- Learn to listen because the ideas you were looking for might just be picked up from the person you are talking to.
- Do not prejudge. A person might be dressed in rags but still keep in his mind rich and brilliant thoughts.
- Even if you find his/her conveyed ideas irrational or senseless, still learn to respect and appreciate. No idea is ever wrong or right. It only depends on one's perception.

So the next time you exchange a conversation with someone, and your subconscious mind starts rejecting the thought, discipline yourself. Appreciate, value, and respect the idea of your neighbor.

Assess consequences of actions or ideas

Look before you leap. Yes, it is also a way of developing your critical thinking skills. Always assess the consequences of actions and ideas. You have definitely heard in the media many stories that ended up in tragedy simply accounting to this lesson. In fact, most failures occur because of the failure to assess actions and ideas before they are made. Regret always happens in the end and none of us would want regret in our lives. We are the only ones responsible of our decisions and when taken for granted, these could cause damage to many.

Make reasoned decisions

Excellent decision making is a characteristic of critical thinking. Decisions should not only be made promptly, but must also contain acceptable reasons behind them. A good decision is not made in an instant; it must involve supporting details that would qualify it to be reasonable enough. And making decisions is a part of daily life, which is why critical thinking must always come into play. Was there ever a time where you made quick decisions and later on you regretted that certain decision? If only you would have spent some more time in assessing that decision, things would have turned out better. We do not want this to happen again. So the next time you find yourself involved in a critical decision-making situation, take note of three or even five reasons why you should consider the decision. If you find yourself lacking in reasons, then perhaps it's not a good decision after all.

Think independently

Letting others think for us discourages our minds to generate wondrous ideas. Over the long term, it will be a bad habit. It is degenerative. And if you are this type of a person, start thinking on your own.

Except when gathering information, do not ask others until you come up with an idea of your own, an idea produced by your brilliant mind. Only when you come up with one can you only consult others and ask for their respective ideas. Never be tempted in letting others think for you, no matter how difficult the question is, no matter how good that other person is. You are brilliant. You can do it on your own. Think independently.

Chapter 8: Critical Thinking for Problem Solving

Using critical thinking techniques allows you to take apart complex problems and understand each element, as well as the effects of your ideas on the problem. Most of us can recall from our days in school that a lot of learning once depended on rote memorization. However, when it comes to solving problems, this approach can be a problem. For, in order to solve a problem, we need not just know facts and information, but be able to apply them as related to a situation. This is where critical thinking ability. comes in.

Step by step view of critical thinking as it applies to problem solving

Identify the Problem

In order to attempt to solve a problem, you must know whether there really is a problem. This means, taking the time to look at a situation and see whether it is a problem that is worth your time and effort to rectify, or whether there has just been some kind of misunderstanding. When you do locate a problem, you need to identify what exactly it is in detailed and specific terms.

Analyze the Problem

Once you know what the problem is, look at it from many different points of view. This will help you to answer questions such as: Can it be solved? Will you be able to solve it alone or will you need the help of others? Is the problem real, or is it only being perceived in that way?

Brainstorm

In this step, you will review your options as far as solutions to the problem. Every problem can be solved in more than one way. Brainstorm a list with as many solutions that you can think of, making a note of whatever comes to mind. Then narrow your list down to the best and most appropriate possible solutions.

Decide on a Solution

Take another look at your list of possible solutions and take your time in deciding which one of them will work best for the problem that you are dealing with.

Take Action

Now that you have carefully reviewed the problem and decided on a solution, it is time to put your plan into action.

Every problem that you solve is an opportunity to better your critical thinking skills. Rather than looking at problems that may arise as challenges that are impossible to meet, use this step by step system to break down the elements of even the most complex issue and find a method of approaching it. In time, you will see that not only your thinking skills, but your problem solving skills will have developed.

Strategies to Improve Problem Solving and Logical Thinking

Delve Deeper into the Question

Starting off with a broad question will make it difficult for you to come up with the right answer, particularly when you are thinking critically. Critical thinking calls for you to examine a host of variables, following which you are then able to get to a solution. Here is an example of how you can delve deeper.

Make Use of Diagrams

A picture speaks a thousand words and an excellent diagram can help to accentuate your logical thinking. A great mind that embodied an excellent critical thinker was Steve Jobs from Apple. When sharing information in a presentation, he drew the audience in and helped them arrive at a conclusion by making use of illustrations and diagrams in his presentations.

Attempt Logical Games

There are games that are purely based on logic if you want to arrive at a solution, such as chess and Sudoku. Chess is a great game to play with another person, as you learn to understand how other people think, and how their thoughts affect their judgments. You also develop the skills of strategy and problem solving, as you work your way across the board in an attempt to win the game.

Sudoku is a great game to play on your own, as it helps you come up with different ways that you can reason. Through this game, you learn about solving a problem by getting rid of certain variables, and using the information that you have available to help you arrive at a viable solution.

Consider your Assumptions

You will be amazed at the number of assumptions that you make before you finally arrive at a decision. Assumptions are not based on truth or something that must happen, they are instead our opinions of something that could happen if we take a certain action. When looking to improve your problem solving and logical thinking abilities, you need to be discern when your thoughts and actions are based on assumptions instead of facts. This means that you need to be able to dissect the issue.

Choose the Right People Around You

When you have people smarter than you around you, it is easier to learn something from them, which will help you improve the way that you do things, as well as build on your critical thinking skills. Their intelligence will make it necessary for you to come up with logical ways to interact and communicate with them, which will help develop the way that your brain works as well.

Read Logical Books

Read, read and read some more, and you will be amazed at how quickly you can elevate your logical reasoning. Do not read just any books. Focus on those that will get you thinking, and these books mainly fall into the category of mysteries and thrillers. As you read these books, work on figuring out what could happen by the end of the book. You may need to identify a villain, figure out what is happening with an attack, or simple solve a mystery of some sort. By looking at all the variables, you will find that making a calculated guess is not only possible, it gets easier with time. To perfect this skill, you must keep reading and keep practicing.

Investigate Everything

Every time that you receive some information, take time to do a thorough investigation to determine whether the information that you have on hand is good or not. This is applicable to all information, no matter who the source may be. When you being to investigate in this matter, your brain starts to analyze information in a different way. You will begin to see loopholes in information, and make judgments based on all that has been made available to you. This is particularly true of negative news which may be sensational rather than factual. Problem solving will become much easier, as will critical thinking when it comes to addressing issues.

Use Intuition and Critical Thinking for Better Problem Solving

Intuitions are very important when coming up with the best strategies to address a particular situation. Why? Because these thoughts are often the stuff that you have learned through experience, which makes them very ideal troubleshooting tools.

They are actually products of justified true beliefs, or the things that you already know to be factual. You consider them hunches because there are pieces of information that are still missing, and your mind immediately tells you that it would be a good idea to test them out, or follow them. Combined with critical thinking, your intuitions become very valuable when it comes to observing and solving real-life puzzles. Here's how you can do that.

Think About Where Your Intuition Came From

Since intuitions are essentially knowledge, you have to know where you got them so you can tell if they are appropriate for the situation. For example, if your eBook reader fails to turn on, you have the intuition that it has no power. The reason why you have that thought is that you have experienced this particular gadget, or any electronic gadget, to not turn on when it is not charged. The most obvious solution then is to plug it in to charge it.

Test Your Hypothesis

If your intuition tells you that your eBook reader failed to turn on because it has no power, there are actually a lot of reasons why this happened. It can be because it is not charged, or that it is broken. These lines of reasoning are all intuitions, but since there are two reasons that are available, you have to make sure that you test them out to find out what the problem really is. What you're going to do next is to charge it, and if it still refuses to turn on, then you have reason to think that it is probably because your gadget broke.

Try to See if You Explored All Available Options

From the above example, do you think that the intuitions mentioned are complete for you to reach the right conclusion? Probably not. It failed to mention to check if the gadget has its batteries, and to see if the problem can be easily resolvable by simply changing the battery. Again, you need to test that out to see if that additional intuition is correct.

Outside the Scientific Method

The above steps actually spoke about a concept that you have learned in elementary, which is the scientific method. However, intuition does not only take place in situations that involve physical objects. It can also happen during moral dilemmas, wherein you have to carefully weigh situations in respect to your values. Just like thinking if you should sign a document that would get you employment in a large company that is quite notorious for land grabbing, you have to check what your moral intuition tells you. You may not be able to test them out empirically, but your argument would largely stem from the set of values that you have. If you firmly believe that it is morally wrong to cause anguish to a poor family for the sake of corporate advancement, then you know that it would be wrong to accept the deal.

Chapter 9: Critical Thinking for Better Decision Making

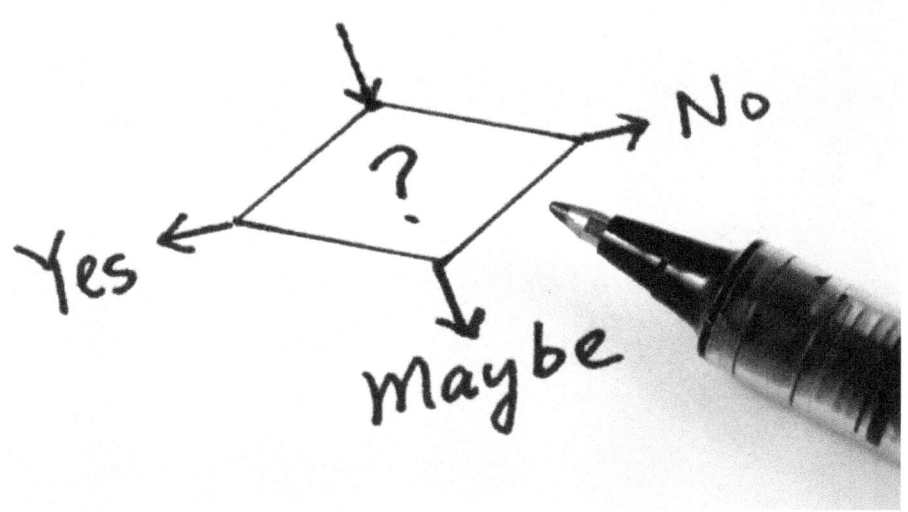

To achieve a goal or an objective, you need to possess decision-making skills. As we have seen, decision-making revolves around making choices and solving problems. This often requires brainstorming and finding out the why, what, when, where, and how as a way to overcome any obstacles that manifest in the course of finding solutions.

Decision-making starts with thinking and then finding out the best way to transform the thoughts into action. Below are some strategies you can employ to improve your decision making skills.

Why decision making is important

Decision making is important because everything that happens to you starts with a decision. The relationships that you choose to form, the job that you choose to work at, and even what day you go to the grocery store are all results of decisions that you have made. As you learn to think critically, you will find that your decision making becomes easier. Rather than reacting based on your emotions or irrational thought, you can make the decisions that will lead to happiness, success and the achievement of your goals.

Don't try to be a perfectionist

Stop trying to be a perfectionist. There is nothing wrong with wanting to do your best. However, you need to know when it is the right time to stop. It doesn't mean that you should settle for less if it isn't the best. It simply means that you should set criteria and stick to it. A perfectionist hesitates while taking the first step and this can be a significant deterrent when it comes to decision-making. A perfectionist always believes that there are only two possible outcomes in any given situation, either success or failure. This isn't how the world works. It is great that you want to be good at something, but it is equally important to understand where to draw the line as well. Don't think that a task isn't completed just because it isn't perfect. Also, this mentality can prevent you from starting something. Not just starting, but even finishing it as well. Instead of chasing perfection, you should focus on being better and completing the task.

Determine important factors first

Have you ever wondered how two people can look at the same situation and come to different conclusions? People develop unique perspectives and conclusions because of their core values and what matters most to them during the decision-making process. This is the reason that you must make your own decisions nobody else can decide what decisions will meet your core values and resonate with your life. Before decision making, create a list of the things most important to you.

Think when your mind is clear

Have you ever agreed to something or been persuaded easier because you were tired? You may not have had the energy or motivation to argue your point or come up with a rebuttal. This is a common occurrence. The research shows that when you do not get enough sleep, it affects your ability to make rational decisions. This is especially true in stressful situations. To keep your mind clear, try to make your decisions after you've had some rest. There must be some truth to the common phrase 'sleep on it' after all.

Be sure you have enough time

When thinking critically about a decision, timing is everything. While you may not have unlimited time for weighing your options, particularly in times of stress or when making business situations, timing drastically affects the critical thinking process.

Timing determines how long you have to gather information and broaden your perspective before diving into the decision-making process. It determines how quickly you must analyze information and look for links between the facts of the current situation and what you already know. Timing also affects the amount of pressure that you feel, which may result in a decision based on pressure rather than one that fulfills the goal of creating the best-case scenario.

Situations will arise where you have to decide based on the limited information that you have. Know all the driving factors in these decisions and be sure that the choice you make comes from a sound place of mind, rather than one that is frazzled with the pressure of making a quick decision.

Listen to your gut

We all have an inner voice that tries helping us in deciding what is right and wrong. However, more often than not, we tend to ignore this inner voice. We ignore it so much that it starts becoming feeble. We are all born with an instinctual compass that can help us determine what the best course of action is for us. This compass is your conscience. Whenever you think you are doing something wrong, don't you feel a sinking sensation in your gut that tells you that something is amiss? Learn to listen to your gut. If you have a bad feeling about something, then it probably is bad. Your intuition can guide you through a difficult decision; just learn to listen to it. In our process of growing up, we often tend to ignore our intuition because of what others say and do.

Understanding cognitive bias

Perhaps one of the most clichéd questions that a therapist will ask their patient is "tell me more about your childhood." Human beings collect their experiences. Depending on whether a particular incident or situation is positive or negative, our minds start creating biases. For instance, if you were ever mugged on a specific street, it is very likely that you will try to avoid that street in the future. Or perhaps you were in a relationship with an unfaithful partner and this will create trust issues and will make you question how faithful any potential partner is. These are instances of negative cognitive bias that your brain develops. Such biases can have a lasting impact on your ability to decide. In the same sense, your brain can favor certain things just because of the positive experience you might have had while growing up. Bias can impair your sense of decision-making and prevent you from thinking rationally.

Choosing your timing wisely

You should be mindful of the time when you are deciding as well. For instance, it isn't advisable that you make a big decision after an argument with your partner. This is bound to affect your ability to think clearly, and you will end up doing something impulsively. We often tend to make decisions when we aren't in the right frame of mind. When you are feeling angry, it is likely that you will end up doing something rashly without thinking things through and without thinking about the repercussions of your actions. Always make decisions when your mind isn't foggy. However, spending too much time thinking or overanalyzing is a dangerous thing as well. When in a bad mood, don't make a quick decision. Sleep on it or spend some time to think it through.

Maximize instead of settling

Many people go with the decision that is 'good enough' rather than making a decision that is going to fulfill all their needs. Maximization is about not settling for what works. It is about looking for the best solution rather than settling for a decision. When we make decisions, it can be easy to limit ourselves to just two or three choices. The reality is that three are unlimited possibilities. If you cannot choose because you are unsure of which option will be best, try to find a solution that creates the important benefits from each of the plausible solutions.

Decide on things that are important

Regardless of your age or profession, you will be faced with numerous decisions every day. However, not every decision needs to be given the same weight. For instance, having to decide the theme for a project needs to be given more weight than the choosing what you should have for your next meal. Learn to differentiate between the decisions that are important and the ones that aren't. You obviously shouldn't spend the same amount of time trying to research about a particular lawn fertilizer when compared to learning about a specific health condition. Learn to prioritize your tasks and spend more time while deciding something of significance. When you learn to prioritize your ability to make decisions, you can divert most of your energy towards things that are worth something.

Predicting the Outcome

Sometimes, it is not until after making a decision that you recognize all the real-life consequences. This is especially true of rash decisions made in the heat of the moment or without rational thought. Rather than worrying about the consequences later, think about the outcomes of each for each of your options before making the final decision.

As you consider the outcome, it is important to remember that every action you take has an outward ripple. Even something that seems simple, like walking your dog to the park, affects the people that you bump into on the sidewalk and the other pets in the park. It influences the people driving cars that have to stop for you to cross the road.

As you consider the outcome of your decision, think about how it will affect you personally. Then, consider how it is going to affect everyone else around you. Be sure to think of the short-term and long-term results of your choice and what obstacles might arise as a result of your decision.

There are some who are naturally good decision makers, some who like surrounding themselves with good decision makers, and others who aren't that good at it. Well, like any other skill, even this can be acquired and developed.

Establish The Facts

Decisions you make should have facts and evidence as their base. If you make a decision without looking at and considering the facts, you will end up wasting a lot of time and cash in the end because it takes effort to deal with the consequences of a bad decision.

Consider Options

When it comes to rational decision making, establishing facts is the first step. The information you get will help you develop different options or courses of action. As a critical thinker, you should never put yourself in a position where you have only one option. You need to develop as many options as you can.

Implement and Evaluate the Option

Once you have chosen an option, implement the option. Decide when the option implementation will come into play, who will be responsible for doing what, and the period for implementing the option. You should also pen down evaluation criteria so that you can check whether the option you have chosen is working out well. This way, if anything is amiss, you can quickly make corrections.

Chapter 10: Rewiring Your Brain and Changing Your Perspective

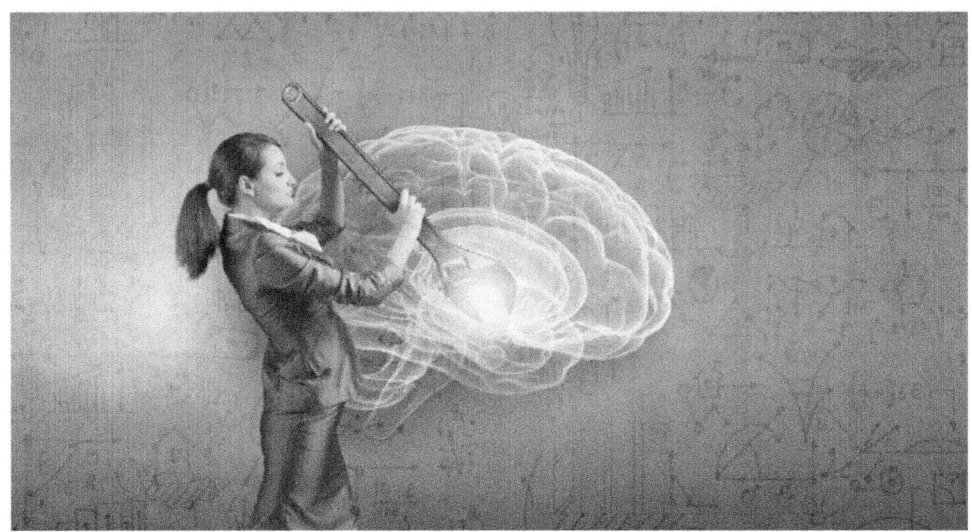

In order to have true success when it comes to thinking critically, you need to be willing to change your perspective on life in general. Critical thinking involves questioning the world around you from the most basic concepts which you hold true, to those issues which may be more complex. If you are doing this, which you should be as a critical thinker, you may find that the way you have been looking at things is not the way you should have been, and of course some rerouting and rewiring of your thoughts will follow.

Changing your perspective on life is nothing to be worried about or shy away from. In fact, you may find that it is refreshing and gives you a new lease on life. You may open yourself up to new possibilities, which you never would have considered before. You may be able to heal a broken relationship with someone whom you had a disagreement with in the past. It can also combat stress, and promotes appreciation of the small things in life. Here are some tips to help you look at things with a fresh point of view.

When you are worried about something, you should ask yourself whether the thing that you are anxious about will matter in five years. You may find that the answer is that it will not even matter one week from now. There are certain decisions in life that will change the course of your life forever, but most of the things that we worry about are not worth the amount of time that we spend worrying about them. Thinking about how much of an impact an issue really has on your life will help you to look at it from a different perspective altogether.

Another way to change the way you look at a situation is by writing about it. If you are not a writer, you can ever draw about it. When you find that something has been on your mind for several days or weeks, the best thing for your to do is sit down and write about it or draw something that represents it. Transferring your thoughts from your mind, to a concrete place can help you to create order out of confusion and see things in a new, and clearer way.

Take some time and write a list of all of the things in your life that you appreciate. This can take a negative viewpoint about your life and transform it into a positive one. From big to small, there are many things that everyone has to be grateful for, and looking at those things, rather than the negative can put everything into a more flattering light.

If you find that it is your physical setting that is frustrating you, going for a walk or going travelling can give you a new mindset. Getting away from whatever you are surrounded by and adding a new atmosphere into your thoughts can be a powerful way to change your life and your experience. Going abroad is especially great, because you get to experience a brand new cultural perspective, which may open your mind to ways of thinking that you never even imagined.

It is All Perspective

People who cannot comprehend why life is worth living are those who easily judge that the situation that they are in is hopeless. When you apply critical thinking, there is no such thing as a hopeless situation – you simply do not know what to do at the moment, but it does not mean that there is no solution.

When people say that everything has a reason, and there is no problem that has no solution, they are telling the truth. Everything that happened around you is an effect of a certain action, which already tells you a clue on how you can better understand and accept things. At the same time, it also gives you the idea that if all the things that you are doing to resolve a problem don't work, maybe you need to stop what you are doing and look for a solution somewhere else. Maybe you just need to ask for help. Or maybe, you can figure it out at a later time, when your mind is not clouded with panic.

Not Exactly Positive Thinking

By looking at problems and situations without judging them right away or generalizing, you are able to see what you really are trying to resolve, which makes a majority of your problems easier to solve. You may even find out that you are facing something that someone else should address.

Critical thinkers automatically become much happier people because they do not burden their emotions and thinking with the utterly useless sensation of worrying. Actually, there is no point in worrying when you try to be logical – you cannot possibly become really burdened by a problem that you can or you cannot solve. You just need to make the most appropriate action based on your resources, reasoning, and values.

That light perspective on life is not exactly positive thinking, but rather, seeing things the way they really are. That means that when you argue and examine claims, you already know that you would not be feeling down about the world. You become aware of what you need to do, and that makes you feel empowered.

Brain Power Strategies To Increase Critical Thinking Abilities

Critical thinking is not something that you can develop overnight, but it is a skill that everyone can start learning in no time at all. If you want to develop your critical thinking, doing the following will greatly help you.

Making sure that your mind has clarity.

You sometimes feel that there is too much going on, and you can't make a decision right away and focus on the tasks that you are supposed to handle. If you think that your brain is handling too much, it would be good for you to take a break. Relax and close your eyes, and imagine that every thought disappears from your mind. Afterwards, try to remember your goals for the day. That would instantly make you remember all the steps that you need to take in their particular order to finish tasks and make planned decisions.

List the pros and cons of a specific action.

If you need to decide on anything, take the time to first think the consequences of your action. Some people think that it helps them when they write the benefits and drawbacks on a piece of paper so that they can see how many reasons can they provide why they should or should not do something.

Make sure that you are always in shape.

You may not notice it, but your health actually dictates how you should feel or think about particular situations. You would notice that when you lack sleep and that you haven't eaten for the entire day, you feel more emotional and you tend to decide to do reckless things. The reason for that is the abnormality that poor health does to your hormones. The same happens when you are extremely tired. If you do not have much energy, you would want to choose what is most convenient, which is, more often than not, not the right thing to do. How do you avoid this? Make sure that you are on top shape.

Always see to it that you avoid bad arguments, and that you detect them.

Bad arguments are probably one of the most annoying things in the world for a critical thinker. The reason is because they are not arguments at all but they are made to persuade or make it seem that an unfounded claim is true. In short, they do not point to the truth, but they are trying to establish something without proper basis. The only good thing about them is that they can

Think outside the box.

Critical thinking, contrary to popular belief, would actually encourage you to be creative. The reason for this is because being able to think outside the traditional norms would lead you to a lot of other perspectives available. When you think outside the box, you are able to have more choices available, and then you can choose which is the most efficient or appropriate action.

One of the best exercises to do this is to think what a friend would say when you do a particular action, or how he would have probably acted in a particular situation. You would be surprised to see that when you assume the role of somebody else, you are likely to look at your situation more objectively.

Having an Open Approach

Having an open mind goes hand in hand with changing your perspective. As a critical thinker, you should never be closed-minded. This can cause you to make decisions without using reason, which of course would not be critical thinking. Besides being open to looking at life through different perspectives, there are a few things to do to make sure that you always approach every situation with an open mind.

First of all, you should never be afraid to accept or understand a concept that may be strange or foreign to you. Just because you do not know about something or have never heard of it does not mean that it may not be the best way to look at things. In order to help with that, you can try to open yourself up to new experiences and opportunities every day.

For instance, something as small as walking a different way to work, or accepting a friendly invitation to a casual outing with someone outside of your sphere of friends can help you to embrace the unknown. Take a class in something that you have no idea about, or eat at a restaurant that serves an unfamiliar cuisine. Open yourself up to the world.

In this respect, do not form negative opinions about something without enough knowledge or evidence with which to support them. Also try saying "Yes" more, instead of turning things down without a second thought. Do not be afraid to step outside of your comfort zone, as you never know what lies outside of it. As a critical thinker, the more things you know about the better, so do not bar yourself from expanding your sphere of knowledge and experience.

Just like changing your perspective, opening your mind can be helped by traveling more. Even if you have a limited budget, try going to someplace that you have never been, whether it is for a few months or just a few hours. If that is outside of your range of expense, you can start off by watching the travel channel, or reading books about places that you have never experienced for yourself.

The bottom line is, having an open approach starts with trying new things. Once you are no longer afraid of what you do not know, you will be more likely to come to situations or problems with an open mind. This will without a doubt, lead to you making the best decision that you possibly can.

Chapter 11: Critical thinking and Goal Setting

Keep a simple thing in mind before learning about setting goals: Do not worry for even a minute if your objective seems irrational to others. It doesn't matter. Well, if it doesn't scare you a little, it isn't worth doing. Also, the crazy ideas are the ones that can revolutionize the world. Here are certain things that you should keep in mind while setting goals for yourself.

Always start with the ideal situation

Here's your chance to dream. Imagine that you have a blank slate and you get to decide who you can be what you want to do. Don't worry about the obstacles immediately, just start with your dreams. There may be various things that you want to do in your life. Start with the possibilities and then you can move onto the practicality of your idea. Yes, don't worry about the bills, the mortgages, or other burdens while dreaming. Think about the ideal version of "you" and then you will have to think of how you can make it a reality.

Always write down your goals

When you start writing down your goals, you will start seeing the direction you want to head in, and this makes the process of decision making quite simple. This might sound old school, but writing down your goals is very helpful. People usually like keeping everything in their brain instead of writing it down. When you write something down, it provides a sense of clarity.

Once you have written your goal or goals down, you should place that paper in a place where you will see it daily. Place a copy of it in your refrigerator or the mirror. This will act as a reminder and will encourage you to think about your goal. This form of repeated exposure helps in focusing your conscious and subconscious mind on what you want to achieve.

Determine its importance

You need to be clear when it comes to setting your goals. Why is the goal essential for you? Is it important because your family wants you to do it or because you want to? Your goals shouldn't be the "should be" ones. Well, there are plenty of things that you "should be" doing according to others and the society that we live in. Instead, think about the things that you want to do.

Your goals should add some meaning to your life

Your goals should never be vague. A vague goal can derail your faster than anything else. If you want to become a better basketball player, exercise frequently, or become a better leader, then your goal needs to be certain. Announce your goal and be honest with yourself about whether it lends a sense of clarity or not. Once your goal is clear, then you need to make sure that it is something that you care about and not what others around you care about. Many goals might seem specific, but they, in fact, are quite vague.

Prioritize and pursue your goal

It is very likely that you will have plenty of important things in your life. So, make a list of all your goals and then select the three most important goals from that list. These three would make up your tier-one goals: the ones that have the potential of altering your life drastically. They aren't necessarily the goals that will help you in minting money or earn you fame, but they are the goals that will lend some meaning to your life. These goals can be big or small and could be something like changing your profession, completing your college, or paying off your student loans. The only condition is that the goals mentioned in tier-one should be of some significance to you.

Setting a target date

This is one of the toughest steps, but you need to do it. Listing down a specific goal is just one step, but that doesn't mean anything if you don't create a deadline for yourself. For instance, a goal that says, "I want to lose 15 pounds" is a specific goal but something that says, "I want to lose 15 pounds within three months" makes your goal seem actionable. It gives you a target to work with. When you don't set a deadline for yourself, it is very likely that you will end up procrastinating. Procrastinating is a fundamental human tendency and, without a target, you wouldn't achieve your target. And not just that, having a target also allows you to measure your progress and adjust the pace at which you are going.

Taking small steps

You don't need to do everything at once. Take it slow and steady. Once you have managed to finalize on a goal that is not just important to you, but excites you as well, the next step is to start taking small steps that will help you in achieving your goal. You can create a one-step-a-day rule for yourself. This means that every day you will be doing something, regardless of how small or significant it is, that will help you in achieving your goals.

Less is more

The more goals that you have, the less time and energy you will have at your disposal for each one. So, it would be wise to limit the number of goals that you have set for yourself. One single goal would be great because it means that you will be able to dedicate all your time, energy, and focus towards that one goal. Every aspect of your life like health, career, education and so on can be goal oriented, but you will indeed be spreading yourself to think if you try this approach. Try working on one goal before moving on to the next one. This is the best way in which you can achieve success.

Make a to-do list

Making a to-do list is quite helpful. Take a sheet of paper and list down all the things that you have to do on that particular day. You can either do this as soon as you wake up in the morning, or you can make your to-do list on the previous night before going to bed. So, when you wake up in the morning, you will have a sense of direction, and you will know what needs to be accomplished by the end of the day. A to-do list also helps in relieving your anxiety about a particular task. A to-do list is convenient, and it will help in making sure that you don't forget anything.

Option to go public or staying private

Well, do you want to tell others about the goals you have set for yourself? The answer to this question depends on whether the added pressure will help you or just hinder your progress. When you start telling others about your goals, you start making yourself accountable to others, and this can help you in achieving your goals. But it certainly doesn't make the process more enjoyable. If you like working on your own and you like keeping things to yourself, then you don't have to announce your goals to the rest of the world.

Plan of action

Once you have decided the goal for yourself, you will need a plan of action that will help you in achieving that goal. A goal without a plan of action will not get you too far. It is all well and good that you have set a goal for yourself, but what good is that goal, if you don't know how to achieve it? You don't need to know all the steps beforehand. But you certainly should know the step that you should be taking at present to bring yourself a bit closer to your goal. Spend some time and create a plan of action for yourself. Learn to plan your day so that you are making the most efficient use of the time that's available to you.

Adjust and adapt

You can indeed have a specific goal for yourself, and you would have created a strategy for yourself that will allow you to achieve the goal you want. Well, your approach should allow for changes and adjustments. At times you will have to reevaluate plans, retrace your steps, and overcome certain obstacles that you couldn't foresee. All these things will take up extra time and might delay the attainment of your goals. So, leave some space in your plans for adjustments and adaptations.

Chapter 12: Critical Thinking and self-improvement

Those actively engaged in critical thought learn the importance of planning. Critical thinkers improve their lives by:

- Spending time reflecting about where they have been and what they have accomplished, and then thinking about what they want to achieve in their life.

- Thinking about and planning for the obstacles that may stand in the way of achieving their goals. Some of those obstacles may be internal to them (lack of motivation, fear), and some may be external (lack of financial resources, lack of education).

- Figuring out the various options that they can utilize to work through, or work around the various obstacles that lay before them.

- Prioritizing their goals in terms of their relevance toward self-improvement.

- Designing measurable objectives for each specific goal that, when accomplished, will carry them that much closer to achieving their goal.

- Setting aside time to plan every day in order to map out tasks they need to accomplish that day to complete their objectives.

- Anticipating distractions that will come up in their daily work and planning for those distractions accordingly.

- Regularly reassessing and reevaluating goals to validate their relevance.

Reflection

At the end of each day, critical thinkers take the time to reflect on how they managed their time and their tasks and then consider that information as they plan for the next day. Here is a list of questions you may ask yourself during your reflective time:

- What was the most satisfying part of my day today and what made it so satisfying?

- What was the most disappointing part of my day today and what could I have done to make it more successful?

- What did I accomplish today that served to push me further on toward accomplishing my goals?

- What did I learn today and how can I use my new knowledge to improve my life, or someone else's life?

- What did I do to help someone else today?

- What events, thoughts, or feelings made me anxious or stressed today and how well did I counteract that stress using my thought processes?

- What did I fail to accomplish today?

- How did my activities today reflect my core values and my goals?

- By doing what I did today, what did I consciously choose not to do?

Short-term versus Long-term Gratification

Long-term gratification is the ability to delay what you want in exchange for a greater reward down the line. The ability to delay gratification is exemplified by the ability to set long-term goals and plan accordingly for them. In order to illustrate the power of long-term gratification, let's look at a study that was conducted at Stanford University for the first time in the late 1960s and repeated to establish validity.

The important thing to remember here is that you can train yourself to delay your gratification. It is not an easy challenge, especially when you have spent your life depending on short-term gratification, but it is possible using self-discipline, motivation, and a plan. Your plan should involve learning, realizing, and practicing delayed gratification every day, and rewarding yourself when you are successful.

Systematic Decision-Making

Determine your core values and your purpose. Ask yourself what principles you want to live by, as well as what you believe to be your life's purpose. These questions are not always easy to answer, but you must at least begin to understand the answers to them before you can effectively move ahead with any important decision-making.

Based upon your values and your life's purpose, determine your goals and your needs. All decisions you make should help you create opportunities and remove impediments that could stand in the way of getting your needs met, accomplishing your goals, and achieving your life's purpose.

Attack the decisions you have to make one at a time, whenever possible. Articulate your problems and possible solutions as clearly and as precisely as possible in order to maximize your understanding of them.

Actively think about and study the circumstances surrounding each problem and each possible solution so that you can clearly understand the issue with which you are dealing. Then, think about the implications, or consequences, of each possible decision you are considering. Separate the decisions over which your control is limited from those where you can exercise more control. Prioritize your problems in such a way that you are focusing on those that will have the greatest impact on accomplishing your goals, needs, and purpose.

Figure out the information you will need in order to make your decision and figure out how you will get that information. Then, work diligently to gather that information.

After you have gathered all relevant information regarding your problem, it is time to analyze the information and evaluate its usefulness toward solving your issue. Separate all factual information from the opinions of others. While you will not discount the non-factual material, you will formulate questions about it regarding possible bias on the part of the people presenting it.

Chapter 13: Critical Thinking and Leadership

One might assume that our leaders in government, in business, and in the nonprofit sector are strong critical thinkers. Sadly, this assumption is largely incorrect. While many leaders have at least some of the qualities of critical thinkers, few possess all of them. However, if one aspires to attain a leadership position at some point, or if one is already a leader within a field and desire to improve leadership skills, one could benefit significantly from studying and applying critical thinking skills in his life.

One of the most important characteristics of a successful leader is that he is constantly striving to learn more about himself and to seek self-improvement. Leaders must know their strengths and their weaknesses so that they can capitalize on what they do well and work to correct areas in which they fall short. Leaders, like critical thinkers, understand that introspection and reflection are life-long processes that must be done routinely and honestly in order to keep oneself sharp.

The second skill a leader must have is that he must be proficient using the tools and the skill sets that he has. In other words, a strong leader must know how to get things done on a daily basis, using the skills he has acquired throughout his life and his training, as well as the tools available to him, technical and otherwise. Leaders, like critical thinkers, must know what they need in order to get the job done. And, just as important, they must know where to look to get what they need in order to accomplish that specific mission. Like critical thinkers, leaders are not afraid to consider various perspectives in order to solve the often-complex problems that they must address. They will seek out others' opinions, and then take the necessary time to examine the quality of each perspective, taking the time to separate the facts from the opinions. Then, and only then, are leaders able to put themselves in a much stronger position to begin to tactfully prepare a strategy to solve the problem.

The third principle of a strong leader requires leaders to develop a sense of responsibility among subordinates. Leaders engaged in the process of critical thought understand that team-building is a very important function of leadership and the best way to accomplish that goal is by working to instill a sense of comradery among those being led. This is accomplished by understanding the mission of the team as well as taking the time to learn the individual strengths of each team member and what they can contribute to the team. Then, the leader must facilitate communications among team members that focuses on information-sharing and breaking down the barriers to honest communication.

A fourth principle is that leaders must be able to make sound decisions in a timely manner. This is without a doubt one of the most important tasks in leadership. As we have learned while studying the decision-making process in our examination of critical thought processes, making a decision begins with a clear and precise statement of the problem. Then, leaders must figure out how and where to gather the information that is necessary in order to begin to think about possible solutions to the problem. Once the information has been collected, leaders must separate the facts from the perspectives and carefully consider each piece of data based upon its own merits. Once the evidence has been evaluated, then the leader must construct possible solutions and consider the likely consequences, or implications, of each possibility. Then, the leader is able to move forward with a decision and take action. This is the same process taken by practicing critical thinkers as they approach problems.

Timely decisions are important because leaders are often called upon to make difficult decisions within a very short amount of time. Even when time is short, it is important for leaders, and for critical thinkers, to make every effort to keep their mission in perspective and work as quickly as possible while working to minimize the possibility of compromising the fundamentals of sound decision-making.

A fifth principle of leadership requires leaders to always focus on setting a positive example. Leaders and critical thinkers best set examples by role-modeling examples of integrity and discipline. Leaders who practice the principles of critical thought are in an optimal position to positively affect those whom they lead because through example, they have the opportunity to motivate people to be both strong critical thinkers AND strong leaders! Leaders set examples by behaving in ways that they wish their subordinates to behave, and they are wise to remember that their position as leaders carries with it an awesome responsibility to teach, as well as to lead.

A sixth principle of leadership requires leaders to know the people they are leading and to look out for their welfare, which aligns with the concept of empathy as we have discussed it in the context of a quality of a critical thinker. Leaders are at least in part responsible for those they lead. That role of responsibility may certainly be enhanced in a military environment, for example, but all leaders are at least in part responsible for educating, training, or assisting their subordinates get from Point A to Point B in some fashion. A strong leader seeks to understand those he leads from their perspective as much as that is possible and he works to accomplish that by holding individual or group meetings with them and by actively listening to what they are saying.

A seventh principle of leadership reminds leaders to keep their people informed. Effective communication is absolutely critical in leadership roles and leaders must make sure that the messages they impart to their crews are clear and precise with minimal or no use of vague or ambiguous terms or phrases. Communications should be delivered in a timely manner. When preparing communications, it is important for the leader to consider his biases that may influence what he says or how he says it. He also needs to consider possible biases held by his team members and how those biases may influence their interpretations of the message he is presenting.

An eighth principle of leadership advises leaders to seek responsibility and to take responsibility for one's actions. In terms of critical thinking, this principle addresses the goal of self-direction and self-accountability. Leaders and critical thinkers are charged with offering their talents and their skill sets when they believe it is appropriate to do so, and they don't wait to be spoon-fed information when they need to solve a problem. They find out where to look and then they gather and analyze the data in a timely fashion. They also take responsibility for their shortcomings as well as their successes.

A ninth principle of leadership requires those who lead to make sure that their assigned tasks are understood and that members of their teams get the supervision they need in order to accomplish tasks successfully. This principle addresses the need for clear and precise communication and the need to understand the perspectives of the people charged with getting the job done.

Chapter 14: Powerful Strategies to Improve Critical Thinking

Keep a Journal

Keeping an intellectual journal can also help you to stick to your goal of improving our critical thinking skills. You can write an entry every day in order to keep your entries regular. Each day, write an entry describing a situation that was or is significant to you. Keep track of different problems that you have managed to resolve as a result of critical thinking. You need to have a format that you can follow to address each problem.

Solve a Problem Each Day

Another strategy that can help you to improve your critical thinking skills is attempting to solve at least one problem a day. In other words, when you start each day, you can choose a problem that you will work on in your free time. Then, take some time to look at the problem from a logical point of view by taking note of all of its elements.

Redefine Your Viewpoint

Being open to considering alternative views about a situation can help you to develop more refined and informed opinions. It may be hard to accept the fact that the the way that you see things currently might need to be adjusted, but it can help in the long run.

Question the Viewpoints of Others

This strategy is not about being an argumentative person, and challenging people openly, especially in situations where this would be inappropriate. Rather, when you are listening to someone speak, do not always accept that the information that they share is a fact.

Take Out Time

You must invest quality time into perfecting your critical thinking time. This does not mean that you set aside hours each day to think. It does mean that when you have a moment, for example, when stuck in traffic or walking from one place to another, take that time to be more productive with your thinking. As you do this, you will begin to observe certain factors about your thought process and how you arrive at conclusions.

Deal with One Problem at a Time

Critical thinking requires your mind to be clear, so do not clutter it with trying to solve too many problems at the same time. Instead, go through one problem at a time. Doing this will enable you to clearly state the problem in your mind and understand what type of problem it is.

Change Your Perspective

It is highly likely that you have a way of being and seeing, which is based on your personal and social interactions. From your experiences, you define the way that you understand things. For normal thinking, this is fine, yet for a critical thinker, this can be very limiting. You will find that seeing the world from one perspective means that your solutions to problems tend to also follow one pattern. Often, this can lead to frustration and negative emotions. A critical thinking needs to be able to redefine how they view the world, so that they have a more open mind. This will make it possible to find solutions in unlikely places or scenarios.

Always Question Assumptions

It's easy to come to the wrong conclusions by just forgetting to question the assumptions you have already made. Some of the best innovators in the past were the people who just wondered if some of our fundamental human assumptions might be wrong.

Acknowledge the Influence of Groups

Groups have an unwritten and sometimes written code of conduct. Groups expect members to do and not do various things. In fact, some groups take their beliefs very seriously and any member who goes against those beliefs is expelled from the group's fold.

Group thinking is a major hindrance to critical thinking. You must guard against it. You can guard against it by acknowledging the influence of groups. Analyze the group you are in, and determine what actions or behavior the group and its members expect you to conform to because every group requires some measure or level of conformity.

Take A Breath, and Have a Thought

Begin to take even a moment before you answer a question, decide on a course of action, or make a decision. Train yourself to think carefully—even briefly—about what you are doing and why you are doing it. The world and people around us seem to move faster by the day, but building critical thought into your everyday life can be revealing as well as productive.

Talk to Yourself

If you find yourself nodding or shaking your head at something said during a conversation or on the news, step back and consider why you made that gesture. What are you agreeing or disagreeing with? Have you always felt that way? When was the last time you thought about the thing you are agreeing or disagreeing with as a topic of consideration—rather than something you simply agree or disagree with?

Practice asking critical questions

When do you think you would receive the best answer to a question? Would it be when you ask a general question, or when you ask a specific question? And when would you expect to receive a serious and helpful answer? Would it be when you ask a question in a serious manner, or when you ask it in a casual manner? If you want to receive the most helpful answer to a question, the manner of asking matters a great deal. It is important that you tailor your questions in a way that is bound to provoke the person you are addressing into giving you relevant answers that are also helpful. Also when you are trying to design questions that will help you during the time of doing research, it is important that you frame those questions in a manner that will lead them to sources relevant to the issue at hand. You are also able to locate relevant material faster.

Get verifiable evidence

It is recommended that you get into the habit of learning and supporting your ideas by way of evidence that is verifiable, and also by way of logical thinking.

Ask Questions

You may get lost when you are trying to think critically. You may ask so many questions that you don't even know what questions you asked originally. It's like the black hole of critical thinking. This can be exhausting and discouraging. But don't stop! Go back to the basic questions and write it all down. If you write it down, the paper will remember for you.

Be Aware of Your Mental Processes

Self-awareness, self-awareness, self-awareness! Being aware of your own thought process is important, especially since it moves so quickly. Keep those cognitive biases in mind!

Form Your Own Opinions

Even if you are wrong, they can give you a good starting point. This is kind of like the thesis statement of your paper. It helps you decide what you are trying to prove but can be totally different by the time you finish your paper because of the evidence you found.

Do proper analysis

It is also a great idea for you to get used to analyzing whatever issue you have before you attempt to make any deductions. Something else you need to do in the same vein is proper reasoning and also proper evaluation of situations and challenges.

Do reasonable interpretation

It is important that you learn to interpret issues at length and in depth, as you avoid the urge to embrace information solely at face value.

Confirm information veracity

You need to always check the veracity of any information you intend to use, even when you have gotten that information from published books or from the Internet. Even if you are picking information from things you or other people have observed, just check it out for accuracy and credibility. Let us just, in fact, say you need to check the veracity of all information you are considering for use at all times. This helps you to have more accurate information at hand.

Deal with Your Ego

Egocentrism can hinder critical thinking. If you are full of yourself, you will shut your eyes and ears to new ideas or correction s. You will tend to justify your actions, blame others, become defensive or point out the 'deficiencies' of the person trying to correct you. Sometimes, we take our egocentrism too far by associating with people who do not challenge us and avoid people who tend to call us out.

Be innovative

Explore alternatives to seek better and new solutions. You can do this through becoming innovative. Do not be afraid to try. Do not be afraid to take risks. Your mind is a powerful tool that can generate innovation. You must not settle in your comfort zone and be contented with what you already know. Also, do not be contented with what the world and the people around you already know.

Have a healthy lifestyle

Now you might wonder why this item appeared in an article about improving your critical thinking. Yes, living a healthy lifestyle is necessary for the mind's improvement. A sound mind must be housed in a sound body. You can never unleash your full potential if your physique is not at its best state of well-being.

Be creative

Creativity is one thing common among great thinkers and successful people. In the real world, creativity is not only luxury, but a necessity and a survival skill. A critical thinker is a creative person. We all use our creativity in different ways, but we must follow a common process. Once the process is understood, you can apply it intentionally at any situation needed. It boosts your creativity and efficiency and it also strengthens your initiative.

Know when to move on

You might be equipped with so much optimism that you always fight for your idea. But if things aren't working out so well, change your strategy. You did not change your decision to reach your destination; you only took a different route leading to it. This is one characteristic very few have. It is called flexibility. People who have this know when their preferences are getting the best of them and are able to re-strategize and change direction. Do not be obsessed over endless possibilities. If you've done a thorough job and things aren't going so well, move on, and still be on target. Having this skill is like having a good map. Now it's up to you to drive your critical mind to your goals.

Diversify

A critical thinker embraces diversity. One of the most powerful skills of a great thinker is the ability to leverage diversity. We are talking here about diversity of thought or the art and process of leveraging and maximizing different ways of thinking. A critical factor to consider is to always recognize where you are strong and where you are not. If at a certain field you know you are not adept, seek others who are. And exert effort in improving this. Listen to their thoughts and listen to the new directions their thinking can provide. Learn to diversify and be open to others' perspectives.

Have an open mind

It is easy to distinguish a close minded thinker from an open minded one. A close minded thinker is not open to discussions and only firmly believes in his or her own set of beliefs and opinions. This is a very unacceptable attitude for one who wants to develop a critical thinking mind. Improving your thinking involves processing new input. A close minded thinker cannot be convinced or reasoned with. Imagine a glass full of water. It cannot contain new water anymore because it is already full.

Resist impulsiveness

Impulsive decision making is what we aim to correct in developing our thinking skills. Impulsive decision making often leads to poor and regrettable decisions. When we are under pressure, temptation arises to make an impulsive decision. Some may reason out that it is better to have a wrong decision than to have no decision at all. Well, that is rarely true. Indecision is an indication of thinking problems and poor decision making skills while impulsiveness only accelerates and assures the consequences of poor decisions.

Eliminate ambiguity

An excellent critical thinker always exercises the power of thought to establish clarity. Ambiguity is a symptom of irrational, incomplete, and sloppy thinking. Now once you experience this state, examine your principles, your knowledge, your promises, and the efficacy of your thinking process. Knowledge is the only weapon you can use to retrieve clarity from confusion and uncertainty.

Be consistent

Improving your critical thinking is a routine to consistently seek problems in your thinking. Being consistent is a good sign of careful and thorough thinking. A critical thinker always applies consistency and logic in whatever that needs to be considered. Inconsistency is just used to obscure the truth. So if you really want to improve, be consistent.

Practice empathy

A critical thinker always withholds judgment until he or she is sure that he or she has adequate information. This is called empathy. You should not judge others until you fully understand the whole situation. By practicing empathy, you minimize the risk of making impulsive decisions and half-baked conclusions. On the other hand, once you have adequate information and you have examined it well, do not hesitate to make decisions.

Know your learning style

For learning to be most effective and conducive, know your learning style. This is the learning technique wherein you absorb knowledge the fastest. For example, if you prefer hands-on experience, then engage in it. If you prefer lectures, readings, and discussions, take part in these. If you prefer group experiences, then go out and find a group.

Eliminate negative talk

Negative thinking is a self-talk-sub vocal conversation by reinforcing critical judgments and attitudes about you. You convey negative images over and over again. Here are examples of this kind of thinking: I cannot do anything right, I must not trust anyone, I'm not as smart as everyone else, I am ugly, I am not loved, and school is a waste of time. When taken for granted, this kind of thinking will influence your decision making in an undesirable manner. This is a serious thinking problem and thus must be replaced by more positive self-talk and self-esteem.

Have the passion to learn

Anything you want to achieve can be easily attained with the burning desire, commitment, and dedication. Passion is the fuel to keep us doing what we must do. With enough passion, you will love your work wholeheartedly since your mind and heart are set to winning your goal. Learning is the key in improving critical thinking.

Improve listening skills

Listening is a very vital skill that we often take for granted. When engaging in conversations, what you hear is what you get. You may have probably been in a situation when in the middle of a conversation, you realize that a person asked you a question that you didn't even hear. Or perhaps you daydream during a classroom discussion. It happens to us all; it indicates our deficiency in this skill. The better you listen; the more information you will obtain. With more information come better decisions.

Always maintain perspective

Maintaining a sense of perspective amidst an important matter is a characteristic of a critical thinker. Do not balance in any situation and always view the matter on a larger scale. Ask yourself this question; is it really as critical as it is at the moment?

Check Your Emotions

Emotions affect how you think. Many of us make spur of the moment decisions based on our at-the-time emotions, then end up regretting such decisions when we rationally think about it later. Some of us go a step further and allow negative thinking to bring us down and keep us from making decisions that will change our situation. This should not be the case. You need to check your emotions.

Develop Intellectual Humility

As a critical thinker, you should take pride in your developing critical thinking skills and strive to become a better thinker. However, this should not lead you to think that you are immune to mistakes. If you develop intellectual arrogance, you will be setting yourself up for failure because eventually, your arrogance will cloud your judgment and you will begin thinking that your opinion is the only right one.

Stay Self-Aware of your Thought Processes

The phenomenon of human thought is pretty impressive. However, the automation and speed of it can actually hold us back when we attempt to think in a more critical manner. Our minds tend to look for shortcuts to figure out what's going on in our world or immediate situation. When we had to fight off animals or hunt to survive, this was beneficial, but now, it can be a hindrance in everyday decision making situations. An effective critical thinker already knows about their own cognitive biases along with any possible prejudices that might be influencing their solutions and decisions. We all have biases, and becoming aware of these is what contributes to critical thinking.

Always Make sure you're Thinking for Yourself

People often make the mistake of getting so caught up in reading and research that they forget to form their own ideas. This doesn't mean being arrogant or too confident, but just recognizing that in order to answer hard questions, you have to think on your own.

Remember that No one is Perfect

It's impossible for a human being to think critically literally all the time, so remember this and go easy on yourself, especially at first. We all have irrational thoughts sometimes. Critical thinking is a tool, not the default way you should experience life.

Chapter 15: Connecting Critical Thinking to Feelings for Greater Emotional Intelligence

Some people think that feelings are the reasons why people make wrong decisions, but that notion is incomplete. Unexamined emotions are among the reasons why people are likely to have the idea that it is alright to do things that they would probably regret later.

Why Are Your Emotions Important?

When you want to be a critical thinker, it does not mean that you have to shut yourself from emotions. Your feelings exist because of your experiences and your instinct, and these contribute to how you can gauge the validity of a particular case. You would not be able to decide to avoid a snake that you see in the grass without the feeling that you are scared of being bitten. That fear actually makes you capable of deciding to avoid a potentially dangerous situation.

At the same time, most of your values and beliefs are probably also based on your emotion. If you tend to argue on the side of wage increase, you probably know how it feels to make less money that is hardly enough to sustain your most vital needs.

Making the Connect

If you want to make sure that you fortify your emotional intelligence, make sure that you develop the ability to keep your emotions in check. You have to understand where that emotion is coming from – whether that is because of a previous experience or instinct, it proves that you have a reason why you feel that way.

Now, are the choices that your emotion is presenting you valid, or is the way that you feel just making you biased? Your emotions will always make you choose an easier option, but analyze if you are getting more rewards than drawbacks when you follow your heart.

When you analyze your emotion and the decisions that you make because of them, you understand yourself better and make better reasons why you choose to decide in a particular way. You do not simply say, "Just because." You are aware that you consciously made that decision, and that it is not just a spur-of-the-moment, instinctive decision. You provided reason to your emotion, and you are aware that you need to follow what your feelings tell you to do.

Emotional Intelligence and Critical Thinking

Emotional intelligence is important for decision making as it is able to predict the success of a business, the happiness of employees and the quality of all the relationships in an organization.

When making decisions as a critical thinker, you need to look at logic, and from this logic, apply your rational and reasoning so that you arrive at the right answer. With emotional intelligence, this becomes easier. Emotional intelligence affects the following: -

Self-Management

Your decision making can be clouded by emotions that are not kept in check. With emotional intelligence, it becomes possible to manage your emotions better. This will give you more control over the decision making process. In addition, when you have to adapt your emotions and reactions, you can do so to ensure that the response you give to a problem situation helps to resolve it, rather than accentuate it.

Self-Awareness

Emotional intelligence makes you more aware of your emotions, and also helps you to understand your reactions. When you understand your reactions, you are better able to identify triggers that can cause you to react in ways that are irrational. As a critical thinker, this is necessary as arriving at a well thought out decisions requires a stable mind.

Empathy

Being able to connect with others on their level, by discerning their feelings, as well as paying heed to their emotions is another result of emotional intelligence. The critical thinker can use this type of feedback to help relate to them in a more effective way, and also create solutions that are mutually beneficial.

Motivation

A significant aspect of critical thinking and its possible success is inner motivation and commitment to the entire process. Motivation is also important in emotional intelligence as it helps you to bring together those emotions that motivate you to take a specific action, and to see a scenario through to the end so that you can achieve a specific goal

Social Skills

Great teams are able to come together due to emotional intelligence. This is because people are better able to relate to one another, as well as develop their relationships and work in a team. When you have to utilize your critical thinking skills in a group, having people who are all on the same page is an excellent advantage.

Conflict Resolution

Critical thinking can be used for solving a myriad of problems, as well as in working out an argument. When you argue using critical thinking, you are aware that there is a point of view that exists outside your own, that you have a purpose for the argument and an audience, and that it is essential to have a central issue that you are dealing with so that you can tackle it with information from key concepts. Factually and logically, this makes excellent sense, though when you input some emotion, you may end up with irrational solutions. When emotions are not well controlled, they can cloud judgment.

However, with emotional intelligence, it becomes possible to control these emotions, mainly due to empathy and being able to see things from various perspectives. This insight means that one can avoid conflicts that arise in arguments, and better negotiate for the desired results.

Chapter 16: How to Beat Hindrances to Critical Thinking

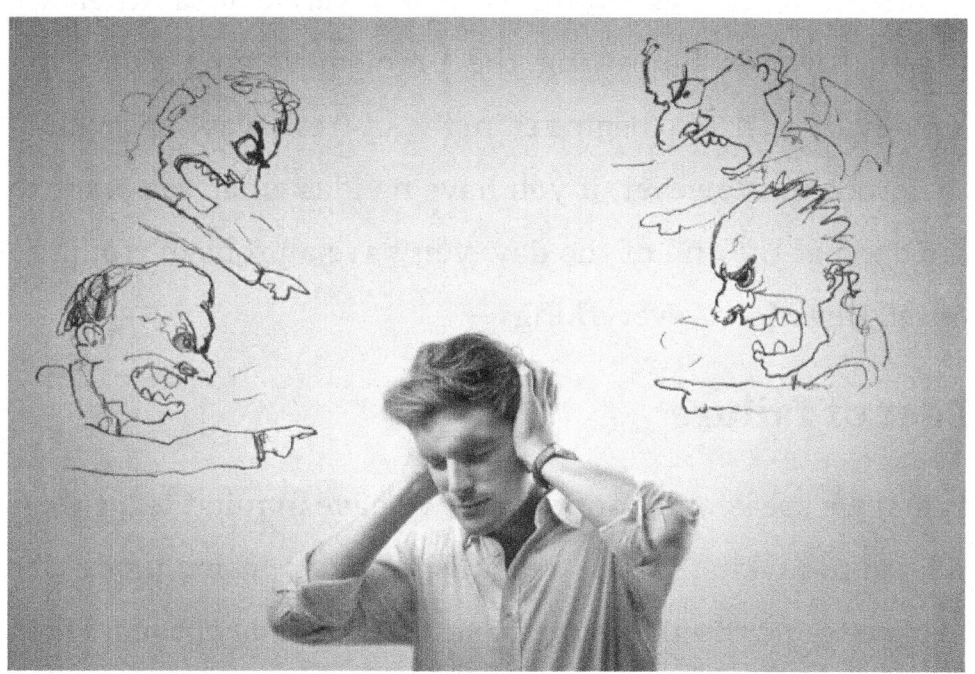

Missing direction

Have you heard people say something to the effect that those who don't know where they are going never reach their destination? You will never know if you are working towards your goal unless you know what your goal is. As such, you need to articulate what your goal is, and then design a plan of action to work towards achieving that goal. Normally, once you see your plan of action well drawn out, your mind begins to work creatively and it generates very innovative ideas that are geared towards improving the problem solving skills you already have. It also begins thinking of fresh ways of tackling the problem. However, if you have no idea what you want to see done at the end of the day, you have a problem from the onset. Direction is everything.

Fear of failure

When we speak of fear of failure, we have in mind fear that is related to making losses, to being wrong, to losing money, to being late and the like. So, you fear that you may not succeed in business, you may lose your investment, and you may not make it in time, and so on. Do you know the part of failing that is worst of all? As long as you internalize the thought of failing, you do not feel motivated, and so you are hesitant to engage in anything productive. In short, you are not eager to begin the problem solving process as long as you feel you are likely to fail at it.

Fearing criticism

When people fear criticism, they also fear ridicule, and, in the same vein, fear rejection. They fear being laughed at. Often, in such cases, the people concerned fear that they may be thought dumb, or make themselves look foolish. Mostly this happens with people who are eager to be liked and to get other people's approval, including approval from people they hardly know; people they hardly care about.

The strife to remain consistent

When you succumb to the urge to remain constant, effectively saying you are going to remain in your comfort zone, you end up getting stuck in a zone with no creative knack and no innovativeness. Before long, you are likely to begin rationalizing not wanting to change, and not wanting to venture out of familiar territory. In short, if you entertain homeostasis, you will be hindering progress as far as problem solving is concerned. This means you are likely to find it very difficult to succeed in business and in any other undertaking you may engage in.

Defense Mechanisms

They are mental processes that occur largely in the unconscious that help us to avoid conscious conflict or anxiety. The major problem with defense mechanisms is that they allow us to procrastinate important problem-solving that would help us tackle the issue that is causing us to feel conflicted and anxious. They are important to discuss in regards to critical thinking because they are mechanisms used by people to distort reality and thus are obstacles to thinking logically, with clarity and with precision. The following are explanations of three of the more commonly used defense mechanisms:

Procrastination

Your goal as a critical thinker is to recognize when you are not being honest with yourself regarding your thoughts, feelings, and behaviors, and when you are allowing your emotions to dictate your actions over what you logically know is the right thing to do.

Seeking justification

How much are you going to succeed in doing if every time you are about to make a move, you halt to explain it to the world? Yet this is something that many people do. You may excuse them once you remember that human beings are basically rational beings, but trying to justify your deeds to all and sundry is bound to make you lag behind. For your business to succeed, and for whatever other undertakings are to succeed fast, you cannot wait to formulate a good reason to give the world, and then wait for the world to give you a nod. You have got to allow yourself room to do what you deem to be fitting without seeking approval from the rest of the world. The security that you seek by trying to rationalize your deeds is a handicap to success.

Enculturation

When you take everything your culture bequeaths you, and you do not care to question it, you are bound to hinder your own progress. Which culture, if you may look back keenly, does not carry beliefs and practices that are not either bare bottlenecks to progress or repugnant to justice? A good number of cultures have prejudices and blind spots, and so taking such practices at face value can be a hindrance to success. You need to ignore those gaps your culture has, set traditional biases and prejudices aside, and embrace critical thinking regardless of what culture stipulates.

The point here is that you have got to be bold enough to challenge the general standpoint and think as an individual who has an independent mind, and who can reason. If you subject ideas - as well as beliefs - to logical scrutiny, you end up purifying them, and implementing them in the form and manner that is most suitable under the circumstances.

Unfavorable emotional states

Who does not value calmness when faced with a challenging situation? Yet, you may often find you are making decisions without weighing how your state of mind is processing the problem. Whenever you make a decision in anger, the facts are likely to be blurred by too much negative emotion, and so the decision may not be the most fitting for the situation. This is the case too if you are depressed at the time of making the decision.

Chapter 17: Keeping the Brain in Shape for Critical Thinking

Which part of your body is most involved in critical thinking? It is, of course, your brain. And for your brain to be in great shape, you need to exercise it, and do it regularly.

Do enjoyable physical exercises

It is advisable to engage in something that you enjoy for an exercise, so that the goodness does not end with your physical state but extends to your mental state as well. Generally what experts say is that by engaging in interesting physical exercises, probably something that you like on the same level as your hobbies, you end up, not just sharpening your mind, but also increasing your happiness.

Exercise your mind

We may have credited interesting physical exercises with improving the mind, but even exercising the mind directly is possible. It is actually possible to improve different parts of your brain by getting them to work, so it is great if you can establish ways of making your brain exercise, because then you will have the brain maintaining the health of its dendrites and its nerve cells. If you are wondering the relevance of those parts – the nerve cells plus the dendrites – they are the parts of your brain that receive information, and then proceed to process it.

Question things

Do you know why questioning is great for your brain? It means you are prepared to search for answers. And just as you do great legwork when searching in the woods or search a vast area, you will do great exercise with your brain when searching for answers. Carrying on your childhood tendencies of trying to satisfy your curiosity is healthy for your brain, and so you need not stifle that natural trait. In fact, you need to deliberately question whatever is happening around you, in other parts of the world, or even the reason for the things that are happening in your life, or those that are affecting your life in one way or the other.

Make a point of laughing

Do you have to listen selectively, so that you only hear things that are amusing? The answer is no. Rather; you need to be able to appreciate the light side of life. Just as they say about the silver lining of the cloud, there should, seriously, be something light about even the most serious of subjects. It does you no good at all, for instance, to frown at food as you eat; chewing as if eating is a continuation of your day job. If you behave this way, you will be tiring your brain and condemning it to a life of dullness.

Feed on Omega 3 fats

The fact that Omega 3 is great for your heart does not mean it cannot be great for other parts of the body. After all, body functions are somehow interrelated. Anyway, the Omega 3 fats do help your heart pump more amounts of oxygen to your brain, and that means better functioning of that organ. That increased supply of oxygen has actually been seen to improve the function of those membranes surrounding the brain cells. Moreover, it is even thought that consuming fish, which happens to be a good source of Omega 3, helps you keep some serious ailments away, such as dementia and depression, and also conditions such as attention deficit disorder, all of which are ailments affecting the brain.

Take a walk down memory lane

It is good to get into the habit of remembering good times because such memories make you happy and, as you have already seen, happiness stimulates your brain and improves its condition, making it function better. To summon great memories, you can, for instance, go through an old album, looking through those ridiculous moments of childhood and youth, and you can also reminiscent about times you were deeply in love when the world seemed at its best. Whatever method you use to recall good times, the positive emotions generated are bound to do your brain a lot of good. Actually, the nice feeling is likely to make any challenges before you appear insignificant.

Reduce intake of saturated fats

What you actually need to do to remain in good health is to consume 30% calories from some form of fat, only ensuring that of that fat, the biggest proportion is from fish and seeds, and also nuts as well as olive oil. As much as possible, you are better off avoiding fats from snacks and fast foods because most of these have trans-fat, which end up raising your level of bad cholesterol.

Solve puzzles

You can rejuvenate your brain by filling out crosswords, solving jigsaw puzzles and such other mind teasing activities. In fact, you do not have to do puzzles that are extremely challenging for them to help improve your brain function. Doing those you enjoy most is sufficient.

Listen to your best music

On this front, do not expect anyone to prescribe the type of music for you. Some people say Mozart works for them, but this cannot be said to be the universal prescription. If you feel that listening to Country music arouses your brain and makes it feel alive, then go for the Kenny Rogers, Charlie Pride, Dolly Parton and the like. And if you want to go the Rod Stewart or Leon Haywood way, it is acceptable too. The point here is, whether listening to Celine Dion or rocking to Michael Jackson, what is going to get you into the groove is not important. Just pick what makes you tick and set your mind free to do its jig. It is healthy and makes you reason better.

Limit your alcohol intake

A little wine may be good for health, but for sure, drinking lots of alcohol is damaging to the brain cells. Binge drinking is particularly dangerous, as it is responsible for killing very many brain cells, and it also deters the brain form forming new cells 30 days after the binge drinking session. In short, in moderation, alcohol is beneficial to your brain, but taken liberally, it can hurt. You need to particularly guard against alcoholism.

Engage in play

Are you familiar with the saying, all work no play? Well, they say it makes you a dull person. This is not an empty cliché. It is actually true that when you regularly have leisure play sessions, like playing cards, tug of war, jumping rope, even playing the child related hide and seek, your brain gets rejuvenated – and your soul, obviously, feels good. On the overall, doing playing for fun and not necessarily for competition relieves you of stress, and it helps the brain function. It even makes you better at thinking strategically.

Allow yourself some sleep after learning

Do you know something interesting about sleep? It does not only give you some nice rest that enables you to think clearly when you awake, it also helps you to retain information. For instance, when you gloss over some key points of a topic just before you sleep, or you actually read something important and soon you fall asleep, chances of you retaining that information correctly in your brain rises by between 20% and 30%.

Concentrate on what you are doing

Maintaining your focus when you are handling a task increases your brainpower. For that reason, you need to concentrate on whatever you are doing, avoiding distractions. You need to realize that whenever you choose something over another thing that was equally important to you, chances are you will be distracted during your chosen task. That means you cannot perform it as well because your brainpower will, most likely, not be at its optimum. Such thoughts of something pending lie just below your consciousness, and you may even try to deny that you are thinking about it because it is not exactly in your consciousness. Nevertheless, they mar your thinking and you cannot think as clearly as you otherwise could.

Embrace love making

Something important you need to note under this point of using love making as a brain enhancing tool is that it does not matter if anyone gets an orgasm or not. The bonding bit that comes with physical intimacy is what counts in improving your brain function. In the same vein, sex need not be sex for the sake of it – it needs to be real love making; an act meant to make the parties happy and closer. That is why women are discouraged from unnecessarily withholding sex from their partners, because it is bound to hurt them as well, denying themselves a dose of natural brain medication.

Put passion into your activities

Can you visualize yourself doing something that you love? Now move a notch higher and visualize yourself doing something that draws crazy passion from you? When you are excited about something you love and you do it with passion, needless to say, the results are normally excellent. It may even be a tough task, but if you are passionate about it, you get an adrenaline rush just by thinking about the chance to do it.

Incidentally, these are the kinds of tasks that also instigate the production of the so-called happy hormones, those that keep your brain healthy and active in a big way.

Keep your focus on the challenge

Of course, it is highly unlikely that you will always manage to come up with solutions for all the problems you try to solve, and that is true even when you come to a problem that is familiar or is similar to another one you handled in the past. The reason that makes every challenge different is that the environments within which different problems come up usually vary. The timing also matters for every challenge that you are faced with. Everything considered, you realize it pays to give special attention to every single challenge as it stands.

Chapter 18: How to Become a Critic of Your Own Thinking

Reliable and sensible thinking can never be discounted. Whether you are a student, a professional, or a housewife, whatever field or industry you may be working in, whatever goals or aspirations you might have, whatever obstacles or difficulties you might be facing, you will always be at an advantage if you know how to employ critical thinking. Feeble thinking, on the other hand, will certainly lead you to difficulties, pains, frustrations, and wasted time and effort.

You may sometimes find yourself wondering, "What is really happening in this particular situation? Am I being taken advantage of? Will I be betraying myself if I accept this idea as true? What will the possible outcomes be if I take this particular action? If I decide to take this particular action, how can I get ready for it? How can I ensure that I will come out victorious in this particular endeavor? Am I really looking at the major issue, or should I be focusing my attention on a more pressing matter?"

Developing this habit of questioning and probing before acting or deciding can definitely send you towards the path of critical thinking. But, you also need to train yourself so that you can be an effective evaluator of your own thinking. In order to become an effective evaluator of your own thinking, you need to prioritize improving your way of thinking.

You can pose these quite uncommon questions to yourself: Have you discovered anything about the way you think? Have you ever observed or studied how you think? Do you know anything about how our brain handles data? Do you know anything about the different processes of your brain, including analysis, evaluation, and reconstruction? Do you know the ultimate source of your thoughts? What is the quality of your thoughts? Do you have more positive or negative thoughts? Do you have any ambiguous, fickle, erroneous, or unreasonable thoughts? Can you fully control your thoughts? Have you ever tested this control? Do you follow any deliberate criterion in determining whether you are thinking properly or defectively? Did you ever become aware of any major problem in how you think and then resolved it by your own intentional act of will? If ever someone approaches you and asks you to teach him or her about thinking, will you have anything to teach that person?

It is essential that you understand that it is very rare to find people who think critically about thinking. This subject matter is not taught in most universities and colleges. Our culture does not actually support this way of thinking. Despite that fact, I am sure that you are aware of the important role that thinking plays in our lives. All the things that we do, desire, and feel are shaped by how we think. It is therefore quite surprising that humans are not all that interested in thinking.

In order to achieve a considerable improvement in your critical thinking skills, you need to prepare yourself to do some intellectual work that many people consider repulsive or even tedious. But, here's the thing: as soon as you start thinking intellectually by moving to a more advanced level of thinking, you will find out that it is not that hard to stay at that advanced level. You simply need to pay the initial price so that you can advance to that higher level.

Don't think that you can become a critical thinker instantly, just as you cannot become a competent tennis player or pianist overnight. To become a critical thinker, you need to have the desire and the willingness to undergo the training required for you to become successful. You should have the willingness to carry out "training sessions" that you may find awkward, demanding, and complicated at first.

Like successful athletes, you need to undergo continuous practice and drills to train your mind to become skilled and competent. If you want your thinking to be improved, you need to prepare yourself to give what other experts in other fields of specialization give—dedication, hard work, and continuous practice.

Here are some techniques you can use in "training" or improving your thinking. These are but a few of the techniques that critical thinkers use to improve their way of thinking.

Always Refine Your Thinking

Don't readily accept the ambiguous ideas thrown at you. Always be wary of unclear, hazy, unstructured, and distorted thinking. Always attempt to work out the practical implications of what other people are telling you. Start by looking at the surface, but don't forget to delve underneath. When you hear a vital news story, try to make out the real meaning behind it. Describe how you understand the issue to another person so that you can refine how you think about that particular issue. Make it a habit to summarize in your own words what other people tell you. Then, share your own version of the issue with the other person and ask them if your understanding is correct. Do not ever consent to or dispute an idea until you are certain that you fully understand the idea.

We frequently believe that our thoughts are understandable to us even when they are actually not. You need to be aware that unclear, confusing, jumbled, misleading, or unreliable thought processes can pose major problems to your life. If you want to become a critical thinker, you need to learn how to think with clarity, pin things down, spell things out, and plainly express what you mean to say. Every time you hear a new idea, try to sum it up using your own words. If you can do this satisfactorily, it means that you indeed understood what the idea is all about. If you cannot do it properly, you may have to gather more information so you can fully understand the idea.

Always Stick to the Point

Be wary of fragmented or patchy thoughts—the kind of thinking that jumps around without rational connections. Be observant and notice when you or the person you are talking to has become distracted and unfocused on the real issue or topic being discussed. During discussions, stay focused on looking for all possible ways to resolve a problem or issue.

If you are a critical thinker, you will stay centered on the primary objective or topic at hand. You will be able to make points that are useful, applicable, and related. You will become attentive to everything that is connected to the main topic. You will be able to reject everything that is unimportant, unsuitable, superfluous, and unrelated. You will know that something is relevant if it can directly help resolve the issue at hand. When you or another person start to drift away from the main topic, you will know how to bring the conversation back to what really matters.

Bravely Question All Questions Being Asked

Be wary of questions being asked during discussions. Be mindful of the questions you ask and the questions you fail to raise. As mentioned earlier, you can start looking at the surface, but an exploration that is limited to the surface is shallow. You need to take time to investigate the deeper implications of questions. Pay attention to how other people pose their questions, their timing in posing the questions, and their failure to ask relevant or important questions.

Critical thinkers know how to consistently pose questions with the intention of understanding and effectively dealing with the different ideas being presented to them. Critical thinkers examine the status quo. Critical thinkers understand that things are frequently not what they seem. The questions critical thinkers ask break through impressions, facades, and half truths. Critical thinkers ask questions that enable the true problems to come out so that they can think their way through said problems and find the solutions.

Be Rational

Similarly, pay attention when other people are being unreasonable. Learn how to recognize when other people are merely using rhetoric to make themselves look rational but their behavior indicates otherwise. Try to decipher why you or other people are becoming irrational. Do you have any vested interests that keep you from being rational? Do others have such vested interests?

Chapter 19: Critical Thinking in Everyday Life

Critical thinking of course is a skill that can be applied to every area of one's everyday life. You might be shocked at the decisions that you can, will and have made which require you to think critically before following through.

You must think critically when doing things such as choosing courses to take on the university level, as well as what major to pursue. Moving to a new place, deciding between two or more job opportunities, selecting a telephone and Internet package, and even planning vacations and other trips, are all decisions that people make every day. Just imagine how much better you will be able to make such decisions, with the power of your developing critical thinking ability. Yes, critical thinking skills are applicable to many areas of personal life.

Of course, our personal lives are not the only aspect of life in which thinking critically is an advantage. Critical thinking will also certainly come in handy when making decisions in the workplace.

For instance, if you hold a position in the Human Resources section of your company, you will be responsible for conducting many workplace investigations. Making the decision of whether to suspend an employee or terminate him, based on his actions has to be based on critical thinking in order to ensure that the right decision is made. Conducting interviews and taking statements from witnesses using objective methodology will help you to gather information and formulate an appropriate plan.

Another example of a position in which critical thinking is beneficial is marketing. Marketing employees can use critical thinking skills to decide how to sell and package products so that the company will be able to generate the most profit. Using assumptions will be a pitfall for someone working in this field. Yet, by using techniques in order to conduct research on a target market and their needs, likes and dislikes will help you to appeal to them so that your product can sell.

Any improvement in thinking cannot take place if there is no conscious commitment towards learning. You cannot improve your game in basketball if you don't put in some effort to do so and the same is true for critical thinking as well. Like any other skill, effort is essential for its development. As long as you take your thinking for granted, there is no way in which you can unlock your true potential. Development in your thinking process is gradual, and there are several plateaus of learning that you will have to overcome and hard work is a precondition for all of this. You cannot become an excellent thinker by just wanting to become one. You will have to make a conscious decision to change certain habits, and this will take some time. So, be patient and don't expect any change to occur overnight.

Making use of "wasted" time

How many times have you been stuck in the rush hour traffic when you could have easily avoided this by leaving an hour earlier? Apart from all the time that we waste doing nothing, we start worrying about unnecessary things. Sometimes we regret the way we functioned in the past, or we just end up daydreaming about "what could have been" and "what can be," instead of putting in some effort to achieve results. Well, you need to realize that there is no way in which you can get all the lost time back again. Instead, try focusing on all the time that you have at your disposal now. One way in which you can develop the habit of critical thinking is to make use of the time that would have normally been "wasted." Instead of spending an hour in front of the TV flipping through channels and getting bored, you can make use of this time or at least a part of it for reflecting on the day you had, the tasks you accomplished, and all that you need to achieve. Spend this time to contemplate your productivity. Here are a couple of questions that you can ask yourself:

Spend some time answering these questions and record your observations. Over a period of time, you will notice that you have a specific pattern of thinking.

One problem per day

Every morning, you should select one problem that you would like to work on during your spare time. Identify the different elements it is made up of so you can figure out a logical solution to it. To put it simply, you should go through the following questions in a systematic order: What is the real problem? How does this problem obstruct my goals, purposes and needs in general? Here are the steps that will help you with problem solving.

Maintain an intellectual journal

Start maintaining an intellectual journal where you record specific information on a weekly basis. Here is the basic format that you should follow. The first step is to list down the situation that was or is significant to you, emotionally. It should be something that you care about and you need to focus on one situation. After this, record your response to that situation. Try being as specific and accurate as you can. Once you have done this, then you need to analyze the situation and your reaction and analyze what you have written. The final step is to assess what you have been through. Assess the implications - what have you learned about yourself? And if given a chance, what would you do differently in that situation?

Reshaping your character

Select an intellectual trait like perseverance, empathy, independence, courage, humility and so on. Once you have selected a feature, try to focus on it for an entire month and cultivate it in yourself. If the trait you have opted for is humility, then start noticing whenever you admit that you are wrong. Whenever you notice yourself indulging in any form of negative behavior or thinking, squash such thoughts. Start reshaping your character and start incorporating desirable behavioral traits while giving up on the negative ones. You are your worst enemy, and you can prevent your growth unknowingly. So, learn to let go of all things negative.

Dealing with your egocentrism

Human beings are inherently egocentric. While thinking about something, we tend to favor ourselves before anyone else subconsciously. Yes, we are biased towards ourselves.

Redefining the way in which you see things

This means that all those situations to which you attach a negative meaning can be transformed into something favorable if you want it to. This strategy is about finding something positive in everything that you would have considered to be negative. Try to see the silver lining in every aspect of your life. It is all about perspectives and perceptions. If you think that something is positive, then you will feel good about it, and if you think it's negative, then you will naturally harbor negative feelings towards it.

Get in touch with your emotions

Whenever you feel a negative emotion creeping up, try to see some humor in it or rationalize it. Concentrate on the thought process that produced the negative emotion, and you can find a solution to your problem.

Analyzing the influence of a group on your life

Carefully observe the way your behavior is influenced by the group you are in. For instance, any group will have specific unwritten rules of conduct that all the members follow. There will be some form of conformity that will be enforced. Check for yourself how much this influences you and the manner in which it impacts you. Check if you are bowing too much to the pressure that is being exerted and if you are doing something just because others expect it of you.

You don't have to start practicing all the steps at once. Start out slowly and try following as many as you can. Initially, you will need to put in a conscious effort for critical thinking to work and, over a period, these skills will come naturally to you.

There is no doubt that critical thinking is a skill that will improve your daily life both personally and professionally, in the long run.

Conclusion

Thank you for making it through to the end of this book. Just because you have finished this book doesn't mean there is nothing left for you to learn on the topic. Expanding your horizons is the only way to find the mastery you seek.

This book has been written to provide an introduction to the process of critical thinking to the reader in order to stimulate interest in a practice that can greatly benefit people as they strive to lead more productive and happy lives. You will eventually be able to trust your own logic and reasoning in any situation, no matter how challenging or difficult. This will allow you to get ahead in the workplace and your personal life.

Utilize all of the strategies that this book has taught you. You have learned how to think like a lawyer, and after this, you will be a problem-solving pro. By following the simple advice that's been provided in this book, you can see a positive change in your productivity and efficiency. You will need to make some conscious effort to start making use of the various strategies mentioned in this book, and you will be able to see a positive change in your ability to make decisions.

Made in the USA
Coppell, TX
18 January 2020

14687224R00134